The
Community
of
NATIONS

The
Community
of
NATIONS

Edited by Mia Adjali
and Deborah Storms

FRIENDSHIP PRESS · NEW YORK

Copyright © 1995 by Friendship Press

Editorial Offices:
475 Riverside Drive, New York, NY 10115

Distribution Offices:
P.O. Box 37844, Cincinnati, OH 45222-0844

Library of Congress Cataloging-in-Publication Data

The community of nations / Mia Adjali & Deborah Storms, editors.
        p. cm.
    ISBN 0-377-00292-5
    1. Christianity and international affairs.   2. Church and
international organization.   3. United Nations.   I. Adjali, Mia,
1939-   . II. Storms, Deborah.
BR115.I7C64   1995
261.8'7–dc20   94-38525
                                                            CIP

Contents

Tables, Lists, and Charts

Foreword

The vision of a peaceful world where lion and lamb lie down together led to the founding of the United Nations fifty years ago. The vision remains to this day despite wars and removal of walls. For the churches, the United Nations with all of its fragility has been over the years that place where nation states sought peace and cooperation. Churches have contributed to the UN and have worked and prayed that the UN might live up to its high calling.

Churches were present at the beginning, contributing to the language of the United Nations Charter. We maintained steadfast support for international cooperation during the difficult years of the Cold War. The churches join with the leaders of the nation states and with people everywhere who hunger for peace to celebrate the accomplishments of the United Nations' last fifty years. In full recognition of the shortcomings, we nonetheless look to the future with hope.

As we look to the next fifty years we are challenged by the action at the World Summit for Social Development (Denmark, March 1995), where 180 UN member states, 118 represented by heads of state, agreed to eradicate poverty. One government after the other acknowledged the need to redefine what constitutes human security. No longer can we guard our borders with arms alone. Only when all people are fed, housed, clothed, and free can we aspire to a peaceful world. The challenge to the UN at age fifty is to discern how to address these issues. The challenge for the churches, especially in the developed world, is how to participate more effectively in this international debate.

Many churches are already involved. About twenty thousand United Methodists will be studying the UN during Women's Division Regional and Conference Schools of Mission. The Presbyterians will hold a Peacemaking Jubilee and the United Church of Christ a pre-Synod Teach-In on the role of the UN. Church Women United, the Evangelical Lutheran Church in America, the Mennonites, and the Episcopal Church are involved in regional and local events. The National Council of the Churches of Christ in the USA hopes to use the results of these events as the raw material for a new policy statement on the United Nations.

This book represents another opportunity for Christians to be engaged in the task of visioning a new future for the United Nations and indeed for all of us. I hope that you will be able to use it to begin discussions in your congregation and your community about the future God wills for God's children. The questions are not easy, and we as North American Christians are likely to find our own comfort challenged.

At the National Council of the Churches of Christ in the USA, we hope to use this opportunity to examine anew our role as peacemaker and our responsibility to the international communities through the UN.

I urge you to join us in that process and to share your visions of the future of the United Nations with others in your denomination and with us.

THE REV. DR. JOAN BROWN CAMPBELL
General Secretary
The National Council of the Churches
of Christ in the USA

A New UN Vision

The National Council of Churches is planning a new statement of its vision of the United Nations and the world community. It is a task that requires the best thinking of all of us. It needs you and the views of your church and others in your community to contribute to the ideas for that statement. The editors and the NCCC Office for World Community hope that you will use this book and its companion, Study Guide to the United Nations, *to do visioning around the tasks of the UN and contribute your vision statements to:*

Office for World Community
UN Project
475 Riverside Drive, Room 670
New York, NY 10115-0050
Telephone 212-870-7376, Fax 212-870-2055.

Welcome to the process.

Introduction

This book is dedicated to those faithful men, women, and children who believe that relationships between peoples and nations can be just and wars can be eliminated as a means of settling conflicts.

> They shall beat their swords into plowshares, and their spears into pruning hooks; nation shall not lift up sword against nation, neither shall they learn war any more.
>
> — *Isaiah 2:4b*

Fifty years ago the United Nations was created as an instrument to develop governments' ability to resolve differences and find ways to improve the quality of life for their peoples. The Preamble to the United Nations Charter proclaims a determination "to save succeeding generations from the scourge of war ... to promote social progress and better standards of life in larger freedom." The preamble refers to "the peoples," not to governments. The success or failure of the UN may rest upon the determination of people to be, or not to be, involved in the affairs of the member governments.

Ambassador Richard Butler, chairman of the United Nations 50th Anniversary Committee, describes new problems in the world and suggests new directions for the United Nations:

> We need to give greater emphasis to the environment than we did in 1945. We need to give greater emphasis to the rights of women than we did in 1945. We need to spread the message and the law on human rights to a greater extent than we did in 1945. We need to address non-military threats to security in a way that we never have done before. We need to accept that more people in this world today are threatened by poverty than they are by guns.

The ecumenical community in North America has chosen to highlight these same priorities in this collection of essays. This convergence of interests could lead to greater interaction between Christians and the United Nations. People searching for appropriate solutions to these concerns often look to the United Nations. Hopefully, Christians will understand that joining this struggle is to be in mission.

The fate of the international community is the fate of each community, no matter how small or how isolated. Every Christian can relate to the concerns of the world. This book and its companion, *Study Guide to the United Nations*, may suggest ways to do so. Peoples' movements and organizations have great opportunities for resolving problems in their own communities and in the world.

The United Nations has found many ways to include representatives of these movements and organizations in their deliberations. Who can forget the thousands of women attending the UN Women's Conference in Nairobi, Kenya, in 1985; or the thousands of people attending the World Summit on Environment and Development in Rio de Janeiro, Brazil, in 1992; or the UN Conference on Population and Development in Cairo, Egypt, in 1994?

It is rare to have a UN Resolution that does not call for non-governmental organizations to participate in its implementation. Ambassador Butler affirms, "We cannot do what we need to have done solely by the action of governments. I have not the slightest doubt that we will only achieve these objectives through the commitment of non-governmental organizations."

The challenge will be to make both governmental and non-governmental bodies accountable to each other and to the millions of people they represent. Can a new community rise out of this collaboration?

Before the birth of the United Nations in 1945, the worldwide Christian community helped to envision a new world order and developed a set of principles known in North America as the "Six Pillars of Peace."

These propositions were prepared by the Commission on a Just and Durable Peace of the Federal Council of the Churches of Christ in America in 1942. They were circulated throughout the churches, with commentary, in a study guide entitled *The Six Pillars of Peace* (single copy, 20 cents postpaid). The *Instruction Manual* for ministers and group leaders was available for 5 cents.

Many churches around the world subscribed to these principles. In Canada, the work on world order was developed by the Canadian United Churches Commission on Church, Nation and World Order. Although wording was not always the same, the spirit was. Yearly observances of a World Order Day promoted activities by the Christian movement toward the creation of the United Nations. Later, it was often celebrated around October 24, the day the UN Charter was ratified. Concern for human rights, self-determination of peoples, peace-building, and development can be attributed to the influence of the churches in the writing of the charter. (See Part One, "The Churches and the UN" by the Rev. Dwain Epps, who represented the World Council of Churches in Geneva and New York for fourteen years.)

Over the past fifty years, the faith community and the UN have seen many obstacles to (as well as opportunities for) justice and peace, as the following pages will demonstrate. This book is not a history of the United Nations, nor

is it a critique. The chapters in Part Two cover six major concerns of the
UN and the ecumenical community — peacekeeping, human rights, women,
children, health, and the environment and sustainable development.

The authors of these pieces take different approaches. They represent
various regions of the world (Asia-Pacific, North America, Caribbean-Latin
America, and Africa) and various church backgrounds. All have been involved with the UN; two work for the organization. They have not tried to
cover all of the issues, but to illustrate particular aspects of the subject that
are crucial at this time. They draw on their own experiences, in the countries
they know best.

Four of the authors are close to the ecumenical community, and therefore
speak directly to that relationship. Dr. Bonnie M. Greene and Dr. David G.
Hallman are associated with the United Church of Canada. The Rev. Bob
Scott (Anglican Church of New Zealand) works with the World Council of
Churches. Cathie Lyons is with the United Methodist Church in the United
States.

Luisa Vicioso of the Dominican Republic and Lindiwe Chaza-Jangira of
Zimbabwe both work for the United Nations. From their experiences with
UNICEF, they focus on the changing situations in the world, the need for
new values and new directions, and the subsequent demands on UNICEF, the
United Nations, and all governments. Both are from Christian backgrounds
and they call the church to action.

News coverage of the United Nations tends to concentrate on Security
Council issues — the wars, the conflicts, the destructive violence in the
world — but not on the often painful struggle to reconcile, to create, to build,
which is 90 percent of the work of the UN and of the churches. As Dr. Bonnie Greene says, "In the world of peacemaking, success is a non-event. It
is a war that doesn't happen, a missile that rusts out before it is used, and
enemies lowering their clenched fists to shake hands."

Clearly, no book can cover all the issues of concern to the Christian community. Many readers in the United States and Canada will be surprised that
there is no chapter on the struggle against racism or against apartheid in
South Africa. We asked Bob Scott to include this grave issue in his chapter
on human rights.

Decolonization has been an important chapter in the history of the United
Nations and the ecumenical community, and we suggested to Lindiwe Chaza-
Jangira that she remind us of the continuing effects of colonialism as she
focused on children in the context of Africa.

The issue of aging also could have been a priority. The United Nations
Non-Governmental Organizations' Committee on Concerns for the Aging
has been chaired for several years by Suzanne Paul, representing Church

World Service and Witness of the National Council of the Churches of Christ in the USA.

Another major issue for Christians has been the situation in Palestine. During 1994–95 the Canadian Council of Churches, the Presbyterian Church USA, and the Episcopal Church USA are part of the North American Coordinating Committee working with the UN Committee on the Inalienable Rights of Palestine.

Other issues that have had much attention from the ecumenical community and the United Nations are the development of the "Law of the Sea," concerns for persons with handicapping conditions, population and development, injustices in the global economic system, global information and communications systems, and the possible need for reform of the United Nations itself.

Several books could be written on the collaboration between the ecumenical community and the United Nations in responding to disasters, participating in humanitarian missions in war zones, and assisting refugees when they are forced to leave their countries as well as when they return. A chapter could have been written on the church as reconciler, as in Central America, Southern Africa, and Sudan.

Our main objective is to help readers find ways to be in mission in the international arena. To be in mission today demands that we expand our neighborhood to include the entire world. Caring about the events in Rwanda and Burundi in Central Africa or in the former Yugoslavia in Europe is as important as participating in the continuous struggle against racism and injustice in the United States and Canada. No one can escape the repercussions from such grave breakdowns in relationships as we have witnessed around the world in recent times. To be in mission is to pursue right relationships, "to love thy neighbor as thyself." Personally participating in the work of the United Nations is one way to do this.

To be in mission is to nurture our communities and the community of nations until all peoples can sit under their own vines and fig trees and no one shall make them afraid (Mic. 4:4).

"Tell me the weight of a snowflake," a coal mouse asked a wild dove.

"Nothing more than nothing," was the answer.

"In that case I must tell you a marvelous story," the coal mouse said.

"I sat on the branch of a fir, close to its trunk, when it began to snow. Since I didn't have anything better to do, I counted the snowflakes settling on the twigs and needles of my branch. Their number was exactly 3,741,952. When the next snowflake dropped onto the branch — nothing more than nothing, as you say — the branch broke off."

*The dove, since Noah's time an authority on the matter, thought about the story for a while and finally said to herself: "Perhaps there is only one person's voice lacking for peace to come about in the world."**

When peace comes to the world — and it will — when racism and exploitation take their place in the past; when nations feed, educate, and heal with the billions now spent on killing; when peace on earth is a presence, not just a song, who knows just whose voice will have been the very last to be raised to break the branch?

Our voices together are hastening that day. And we'd rather that our voices be the first, not the last, to be raised for peace.

The time is one of great opportunity. No dreams of five or ten years ago could have been wild enough to encompass what has already come to pass. From Berlin to Johannesburg to the Middle East, the world has changed in unprecedented ways. Enormous obstacles remain, but persistent efforts of committed peacemaking — around the globe and in our own communities — hold forth great promise.

Perhaps the day will come much sooner than we'd thought. Or perhaps we must be akin to the cathedral builders who knew that they personally would not see the roof in place over their handiwork. Meanwhile, we can continue to add our weight, until global violence finally gives way. Each of our voices, our witness, and our gifts are needed.

THE EDITORS

---

*Adapted with permission from Christmas card of The Fellowship of Reconciliation, Nyack, N.Y.

Part One

FIFTY YEARS

1

The Churches and the UN

Dwain Epps

The churches joined in the ecumenical movement have been at their best at the critical turning points of this century. Often this was a result of the creative give-and-take between a burgeoning international movement for unified Christian action and strong ecumenical organizations in the United States.

Preparing for Peace in the Midst of War

Immediately after the First World War, in August 1920, international church leaders, including the U.S. Federal Council of Churches (formed in 1908), gathered in Geneva, where Archbishop Nathan Söderblom launched the idea of an Ecumenical Council of Churches "which should be able to speak on behalf of Christendom on the religious, moral and social concerns of men."

In 1941, the Federal Council of Churches (FCC) instituted the Commission to Study the Bases of a Just and Durable Peace, chaired by John Foster Dulles, with Walter W. Van Kirk of the FCC staff serving as secretary and with a membership drawn from the most distinguished Protestant theologians and church leaders of the day. The first duty of the Commission was "to clarify the mind of our churches regarding the moral, political and economic foundations of an enduring peace," and "to prepare the people of our churches and of our nation for assuming their appropriate responsibility for the establishment of such a peace." In pursuing their task, they drew upon the work of church leaders around the world.

As we approach the fiftieth anniversary of the adoption of the United Nations Charter, it is appropriate to recall how the Commission to Study the Bases of a Just and Durable Peace influenced and focused international

THE REV. DWAIN EPPS, a minister in the Presbyterian Church (USA), is coordinator of the WCC's Commission of the Churches on International Affairs, based in Geneva. He has served both the WCC and the National Council of Churches in various international affairs positions since 1971. For five years he was director of the CCIA's United Nations office in New York.

Christian social thought in promoting the idea of a United Nations Organization and thinking about what such a world body should do. Its "Statement of Political Propositions," published in 1943, was studied widely across the country, both in church councils and congregations and by political leaders of the day. The principles, best known as the "Six Pillars of Peace," were:

1. The peace must provide the political framework for a continuing collaboration of the United Nations and, in due course, of neutral and enemy nations.

2. The peace must make provision for bringing within the scope of international agreement those economic and financial acts of national governments which have widespread international repercussions.

3. The peace must make provision for an organization to adapt the treaty structure of the world to changing underlying conditions.

4. The peace must proclaim the goal of autonomy for subject peoples, and it must establish an international organization to assure and to supervise the realization of that end.

5. The peace must establish procedures for controlling military establishments everywhere.

6. The peace must establish in principle, and seek to achieve in practice, the right of individuals everywhere to religious and intellectual liberty.

The Churches and the Charter of the United Nations

Almost all of these ideas found their way into the proposals developed in the late summer of 1944 at Dumbarton Oaks in Washington, D.C., where the United States, Great Britain, China, and the Union of Soviet Socialist Republics met to lay the groundwork for a United Nations Charter. Remembering the United States' failure to support the League of Nations after World War I, the Commission on a Just and Durable Peace convened a national study conference in January 1945. The participants issued its "Message to the Churches," which further elaborated on Christian principles and hopes for the charter, including:

- a Preamble to "reaffirm those present and long range purposes of justice and human welfare";
- a special Commission to further the "progress of colonial and dependent peoples to autonomy";
- a special Commission on Human Rights and Fundamental Freedoms, including religious freedom;
- universal membership in the organization;
- limitation and reduction of armaments;
- protection of smaller nations.

Preamble to the Charter of the United Nations

WE THE PEOPLES OF THE UNITED NATIONS DETERMINED

- to save succeeding generations from the scourge of war, which twice in our lifetime has brought untold sorrow to mankind, and
- to reaffirm faith in fundamental human rights, in the dignity and worth of the human person, in the equal rights of men and women and of nations large and small, and
- to establish conditions under which justice and respect for the obligations arising from treaties and other sources of international law can be maintained, and
- to promote social progress and better standards of life in larger freedom,

AND FOR THESE ENDS

- to practice tolerance and live together in peace with one another as good neighbors, and
- to unite our strength to maintain international peace and security, and
- to ensure, by the acceptance of principles and the institution of methods, that armed force shall not be used, save in the common interest, and
- to employ international machinery for the promotion of the economic and social advancement of all peoples,

HAVE RESOLVED TO COMBINE OUR EFFORTS TO ACCOMPLISH THESE AIMS

Accordingly, our respective Governments, through representatives assembled in the city of San Francisco, who have exhibited their full powers found to be in good and due form, have agreed to the present Charter of the United Nations and do hereby establish an international organization to be known as the United Nations.

Edward S. Stettinius, Jr., U.S. Secretary of State, arranged for forty-two national organizations to send representatives to the San Francisco Conference. The Federal Council of Churches was one of these, and it designated Dr. Walter W. Van Kirk, Secretary of the Department of International Justice and Goodwill, as consultant and Bishop James C. Baker, on behalf of the Division of Foreign Missions, and Dr. Frederick Nolde, later to become the first director of the World Council of Churches' Commission of the Churches on International Affairs, as associate consultants.

Through collaboration with other non-governmental consultants, the church representatives were successful in having virtually all of their recommendations incorporated into the charter. A preamble was added along the recommended lines, and more than one observer credited the international Christian influence with having played a determining part in achieving the more extensive provisions for human rights and fundamental freedoms that ultimately found their way into the charter.

The Commission of the Churches on International Affairs

Another significant improvement in the charter was Article 71, which provides for a permanent mechanism of consultation between the UN and non-governmental organizations.

In light of this opportunity, in 1946, the International Missionary Council and the Provisional Committee of the World Council of Churches invited the Commission on a Just and Durable Peace to form the joint permanent Commission of the Churches on International Affairs. Since known as the CCIA, the new commission was one of the first international NGOs to be granted consultative status with the UN Economic and Social Council (ECOSOC).

The headquarters of the CCIA remained in New York City. But offices also were established in London, at the WCC headquarters in Geneva, from which day-to-day cooperation was developed with the office of the UN High Commissioner for Refugees and the International Labor Organization, and in Paris, at the headquarters of the UN Educational, Scientific and Cultural Organization (UNESCO). A commissioner in Rome maintained a link with the Food and Agriculture Organization (FAO), with which formal consultative status also was established.

This deployment of the staff and officers of the CCIA reflected the priorities of the churches immediately after World War II, as they were laid out in the Aims of the CCIA:

> It shall be the task of the Commission to witness to the Lordship of Christ over man and history by serving mankind in the field of international relations and promoting reconciliation and world community in accordance with the biblical testimony to the oneness of mankind by creation; to God's gracious and redemptive action in history; and to the assurance of the coming Kingdom of God in Jesus Christ. This service is demanded by the Church's participation in the continuing ministry of Christ in the world of priestly intercession, prophetic judgment, the arousing of hope and conscience and pastoral care for mankind.... [The] Commission shall: Serve the...Churches...as a source of information and guidance in their approach to international problems, as a medium of common counsel and action, and as an organ in formulating the Christian mind on world issues and in bringing that mind effectively to bear upon such issues; and encourage:
>
> a. the promotion of peace with justice and freedom;
> b. the development of international law and of effective international institutions;

c. the respect for and observance of human rights and fundamental freedoms, special attention being given to the problem of religious liberty;
d. the international control and reduction of armaments;
e. the furtherance of economic justice through international economic cooperation;
f. acceptance by all nations of the obligation to promote to the utmost the welfare of all peoples, and the development of free political institutions;
g. the advance toward self-government of still dependent territories;
h. the international promotion of social, cultural, educational and humanitarian enterprises.

Human Rights and Religious Liberty

The work begun during the Second World War and at the founding of the UN to assure a central place for human rights in the work of international organizations continued intensively after 1945. The CCIA went to work immediately, together with Eleanor Roosevelt, René Cassin, and others, to press for the elaboration and adoption of the Universal Declaration of Human Rights. This was achieved on December 10, 1948. Dr. Nolde and his colleagues had a significant hand in drafting the declaration and provided the text of the article on religious liberty.

Over the years, the WCC, through the CCIA, has been in the forefront of efforts at the UN and in direct interventions with governments around the world to protect the right to freedom of religion and religious expression.

The 1995 UN World Conference on Human Rights, in Vienna, demonstrated yet again that the price of liberty is eternal vigilance, as John Philpot Curran, the Irish barrister, put it in his 1790 speech on "The Right of Election." Each generation must reappropriate human rights as a sacred value for itself and re-equip itself to guard against the erosion of the rule of law as it applies to the protection of the full range of rights included in the International Bill of Human Rights.

Accordingly, the CCIA is now preparing for a second global review of ecumenical thinking and policy in the field of human rights and religious liberty.

A New Turning Point

The UN is at its most important turning point since its formation. With the collapse of communism, graphically symbolized by the crumbling of the Berlin Wall in 1989, everything changed. The end of the Cold War brought incredible new possibilities for the realization of the dreams of a just, peaceful world order. In rapid succession, a series of terribly destructive conflict situations were resolved: Afghanistan, Cambodia, Angola, Namibia, and El

Salvador. The apartheid regime in South Africa gave way to concerted international pressure, and tensions were reduced throughout Northeast and Southeast Asia.

But the "New World Order" (a term coined by President George Bush on the eve of the Gulf War) is often referred to as the "New World Dis-order." Secretary General Boutros Boutros-Ghali's "Agenda for Peace" has become bogged down. UN peacekeeping forces are being sent to many new locations, further complicating as many conflicts as they resolve. At the same time, sky-rocketing costs of these operations threaten to bankrupt the whole organiza-tion. The agenda of the UN is becoming increasingly unclear. As more power flows to the Security Council, and especially to its five permanent members, the vast majority of the world's nations feel increasingly alienated. Pressure is on for a reform of UN structures, but it tends to move more in the interests of the industrialized nations than of the poorest of the world's peoples.

The Vienna World Conference on Human Rights demonstrated that crisis in world order thinking has a clear spiritual dimension, and international policy and politics are more and more infused with apparent religious over-tones (particularly between "Christian" and "Islamic" nations). Ethnic and religious conflicts have exploded in the former Soviet Union and the Balkan region, in Southern Asia, throughout Africa, and in Central America.

The Churches at the New Crossroads

It is precisely at such turning points where the common witness of the churches, new efforts for Christian unity, and increased capacity for interfaith dialogue and cooperation become essential components of, and contributors to, good governance at global, national, and local levels around the world.

With dwindling resources and a turning inward of nations and many of their churches, the question could well be asked: Are the churches and the ecumenical movement up to the present challenge? Or, what are the likely consequences for international justice, peace, and human rights if the churches fail to meet their responsibilities, fail to provide leadership in this critical hour?

Standing solidly on the shoulders of those who have gone before, we must find new vision, take approaches to old issues that present themselves in new ways. The WCC, relying heavily on its United Nations Headquarters Liaison Office in New York, promoted the churches' participation in the implemen-tation of the Earth Charter, developed by the UN "Earth Summit" in Rio de Janeiro (1992), and sought to influence the agendas and make significant contributions to the UN World Conference on Population and Develop-ment (1994), the World Summit on Social Development (1995), and the

Fourth World Conference on Women (1995). Special attention is paid to shifts in UN structures as they affect the opportunities for poorer countries to participate in decision-making and to revise approaches to economic and social development.

New approaches are being taken to the old issues of disarmament, the arms race, commerce in conventional weapons, and militarism. The WCC Central Committee recently created a "Program to Overcome Violence" to assist the churches in confronting the universally pervasive culture of violence and in promoting a culture of peace.

In concrete terms, the World Council of Churches has stepped up its activity in conflict resolution and mediation. It has helped bring together Muslim, Catholic, Orthodox, and Reformed Christian leaders in the former Yugoslavia. It is working to end the war between Armenia and Azerbaijan, bringing together the Sheikh-ul-Islam from Azerbaijan with the Catholics of the Armenian Apostolic Church, seeking to build bridges for peace. It is seeking a negotiated peace in the Sudan. And it is involved in negotiating efforts in Angola, Sri Lanka, East Timor, Guatemala, and elsewhere to strengthen the Christian witness and effective action for peace by non-violent means.

The New Role of International Affairs in the National Council of the Churches of Christ in the USA

This ecumenical journey had significant beginnings in the fledgling U.S. ecumenical movement, was nurtured in significant ways in the Federal Council of Churches, and has been supported and sustained by the National Council of the Churches of Christ in the United States of America (NCCCUSA).

Regrettably, the capacity of the NCCCUSA to contribute to global ecumenical work on international affairs has been reduced to an extremely dangerous point. Like some other national church bodies in the industrialized world, it has allowed itself to become seriously impaired in this essential area of Christian witness.

The role of the United States in the post-Cold War period is obvious, whether as the "last remaining superpower" or as "the most significant voice in world political affairs." The world looks to the United States for guidance in this hour. It expects great things, not only from leaders of government, but also from church leaders and ecumenical bodies. The WCC and its member churches are among those who look expectantly to the NCCCUSA as an informed, expert, active counterpart in the global ecumenical endeavor, most especially in the field of international affairs. A chain without this link can sustain little. But with that link forged strong, as history shows, great things are possible.

2

Member States of the UN

MEMBER STATE	ADMITTED	ASSESSMENT %†	POPULATION (est.)
Afghanistan	Nov 19, 1946	0.01	16,433,000
Albania	Dec 14, 1955	0.01	3,250,000
Algeria	Oct 8, 1962	0.16	25,324,000
Andorra	Jul 28, 1993	*	59,000
Angola	Dec 1, 1976	0.01	10,020,000
Antigua & Barbuda	Nov 11, 1981	0.01	77,000
Argentina	Oct 24, 1945	0.50	732,609,000
Armenia	Mar 2, 1992	0.13	3,376,000
Australia	Nov 1, 1945	1.50	117,086,000
Austria	Dec 14, 1955	0.75	7,823,000
Azerbaijan	Mar 2, 1992	0.20	27,137,000
Bahamas	Sep 18, 1973	0.02	253,000
Bahrain	Sep 21, 1971	0.03	503,000
Bangladesh	Sep 17, 1974	0.01	104,766,143
Barbados	Dec 9, 1966	0.01	257,082
Belarus	Oct 24, 1945	0.48	10,297,000
Belgium	Dec 27, 1945	1.06	9,845,000
Belize	Sep 25, 1981	0.01	194,000
Benin	Sep 20, 1960	0.01	4,889,000
Bhutan	Sep 21, 1971	0.01	1,517,000
Bolivia	Nov 14, 1945	0.01	7,400,000
Bosnia & Herzegovina	May 22, 1992	0.04	4,300,000
Botswana	Oct 17, 1966	0.01	1,348,000
Brazil	Oct 24, 1945	1.59	153,322,000
Brunei Darussalam	Sep 21, 1984	0.03	266,000
Bulgaria	Dec 14, 1955	0.13	8,977,000
Burkina Faso	Sep 20, 1960	0.01	9,242,000
Burundi	Sep 18, 1962	0.01	5,620,000
Cambodia	Dec 14, 1955	0.01	8,246,000
Cameroon	Sep 20, 1960	0.01	11,834,000
Canada	Nov 9, 1945	3.11	26,992,000

*Information was not available or assessment rate was not determined at this date.

†Estimated contribution to UN budget, by percentage of total budget based on a ten-year average of a nation's per capita income. The minimum assessment is 0.01%; the maximum is 25%.

MEMBER STATE	ADMITTED	ASSESSMENT %	POPULATION (est.)
Cape Verde	Sep 16,1975	0.01	370,000
Central African Republic	Sep 20, 1960	0.01	3,039,000
Chad	Sep 20, 1960	0.01	5,679,000
Chile	Oct 24, 1945	0.08	13,386,000
China	Oct 24, 1945	0.77	1,160,017,000
Colombia	Nov 5, 1945	0.13	32,987,000
Comoros	Nov 12, 1945	0.01	551,000
Congo	Sep 20, 1960	0.01	2,271,000
Costa Rica	Nov 2, 1945	0.01	3,030,000
Côte d'Ivoire	Sep 20, 1960	0.02	11,998,000
Croatia	May 22, 1992	0.13	4,700,000
Cuba	Oct 24, 1945	0.09	10,695,000
Cyprus	Sep 20,1960	0.02	707,000
Czech Republic	Jan 19,1993	0.55	15,599,000
Democratic People's Republic of Korea	Sep 17, 1991	0.05	21,773,000
Denmark	Oct 24, 1945	0.65	5,140,000
Djibouti	Sep 20, 1977	0.01	409,000
Dominica	Dec 18, 1978	0.01	83,000
Dominican Republic	Oct 24, 1945	0.02	7,170,000
Ecuador	Dec 21, 1945	0.03	9,623,000
Egypt	Oct 24, 1945	0.07	54,609,000
El Salvador	Oct 24, 1945	0.01	5,252,000
Equatorial Guinea	Nov 12, 1968	0.01	356,000
Eritrea	May 28, 1993	*	3,318,000
Estonia	Sep 17, 1991	0.07	1,565,000
Ethiopia	Nov 13, 1945	0.01	53,383,000
Fiji	Oct 13, 1970	0.01	736,000
Finland	Dec 14, 1955	0.57	4,986,000
France	Oct 24, 1945	6.00	56,720,000
Gabon	Sep 20, 1960	0.02	1,172,000
Gambia	Sep 21, 1965	0.01	861,000
Georgia	July 31, 1992	0.21	5,400,000
Germany	Sep 18, 1973	8.93	79,973,000
Ghana	Mar 8, 1957	0.01	15,028,000
Greece	Oct 25, 1945	0.35	10,269,000
Grenada	Sep 17, 1974	0.01	85,000
Guatemala	Nov 21, 1945	0.02	9,197,000
Guinea	Dec 12, 1958	0.01	5,756,000
Guinea-Bissau	Sep 17, 1974	0.01	965,000
Guyana	Sep 20, 1966	0.01	796,000
Haiti	Oct 24, 1945	0.01	6,625,000
Honduras	Dec 17, 1945	0.01	5,105,000
Hungary	Dec 14, 1955	0.18	10,341,000
Iceland	Nov 19, 1946	0.03	258,000
India	Oct 30, 1945	0.36	843,931,000

MEMBER STATE	ADMITTED	ASSESSMENT %	POPULATION (est.)
Indonesia	Sep 28, 1950	0.16	179,322,000
Iran	Oct 24, 1945	0.77	58,798,000
Iraq	Dec 21, 1945	0.13	18,920,000
Ireland	Dec 14, 1955	0.18	3,523,000
Israel	May 11, 1949	0.23	5,037,000
Italy	Dec 14, 1955	4.29	57,690,000
Jamaica	Sep 18, 1962	0.01	2,420,000
Japan	Dec 18, 1956	12.45	123,921,000
Jordan	Dec 14, 1955	0.01	4,010,000
Kazakhstan	Mar 2, 1992	0.35	16,793,000
Kenya	Dec 16, 1963	0.01	25,905,000
Kuwait	May 14, 1963	0.26	2,143,000
Kyrgyzstan	Mar 2, 1992	0.06	4,422,000
Lao People's Democratic Republic	Dec 14, 1955	0.01	4,139,000
Latvia	Sep 17, 1991	0.13	2,686,000
Lebanon	Oct 24, 1945	0.01	2,701,000
Lesotho	Oct 17, 1966	0.01	1,774,000
Liberia	Nov 2, 1945	0.01	2,705,000
Libyan Arab Jamahiriya	Dec 14, 1955	0.24	4,083,000
Liechtenstein	Sep 18, 1990	0.01	29,000
Lithuania	Sep 17, 1991	0.15	3,739,000
Luxembourg	Oct 24, 1945	0.06	385,000
Macedonia, the Former Yugoslav Republic of	Apr 8, 1993	*	*
Madagascar	Sep 20, 1960	0.01	11,197,000
Malawi	Dec 1, 1964	0.01	8,556,000
Malaysia	Sep 17, 1957	0.12	17,756,000
Maldives	Sep 21, 1965	0.01	223,000
Mali	Sep 28, 1960	0.01	8,156,000
Malta	Dec 1, 1964	0.01	356,000
Marshall Islands	Sep 17, 1991	0.01	48,000
Mauritania	Oct 27, 1961	0.01	2,036,000
Mauritius	Apr 24, 1968	0.01	1,070,000
Mexico	Nov 7, 1945	0.01	87,836,000
Micronesia, Federated States of	Sep 17, 1991	0.01	99,000
Monaco	May 28, 1993	*	30,000
Mongolia	Oct 27, 1961	0.01	2,190,000
Morocco	Nov 12, 1956	0.03	25,061,000
Mozambique	Sep 16, 1975	0.01	15,656,000
Myanmar	Apr 19, 1948	.014	1,675,000
Namibia	Apr 23, 1990	0.01	1,781,000
Nepal	Dec 14, 1955	0.01	18,916,000
Netherlands	Dec 10, 1945	1.50	15,131,000
New Zealand	Oct 24, 1945	0.24	3,380,000

MEMBER STATE	ADMITTED	ACCESSIBILITY %	POPULATION (est.)
Nicaragua	Oct 24, 1945	0.01	3,999,000
Niger	Sep 20, 1960	0.01	7,732,000
Nigeria	Oct 7, 1960	0.20	108,542,000
Norway	Nov 27, 1945	0.55	4,262,000
Oman	Oct 7, 1971	0.03	1,502,000
Pakistan	Sep 30, 1947	0.06	115,520,000
Palau	Dec 15, 1994	0.01	15,000
Panama	Nov 13, 1945	0.02	2,466,000
Papua New Guinea	Oct 10, 1975	0.01	3,699,000
Paraguay	Oct 24, 1945	0.02	4,277,000
Peru	Oct 31, 1945	0.06	21,998,000
Philippines	Oct 24, 1945	0.07	61,480,000
Poland	Oct 24, 1945	0.47	38,244,000
Portugal	Dec 14, 1955	0.20	9,868,000
Qatar	Sep 21, 1971	0.05	486,000
Republic of Korea	Sep 17, 1991	0.69	43,500,000
Republic of Moldova	Mar 2, 1992	0.15	4,373,000
Romania	Dec 14, 1955	0.17	23,201,000
Russian Federation	Oct 24, 1945	6.71	148,485,000
Rwanda	Sep 18, 1962	0.01	7,165,000
St. Kitts & Nevis	Sep 23, 1983	0.01	44,000
St. Lucia	Sep 18, 1979	0.01	151,000
St. Vincent & The Grenadines	Sep 16, 1980	0.01	116,000
Samoa	Dec 15, 1976	0.01	164,000
San Marino	Mar 2, 1992	*	24,000
São Tomé & Príncipe	Sep 16, 1975	0.01	121,000
Saudi Arabia	Oct 24, 1945	0.96	14,870,000
Senegal	Sep 28, 1960	0.01	7,327,000
Seychelles	Sep 21, 1976	0.01	68,000
Sierra Leone	Sep 27, 1961	0.01	4,151,000
Singapore	Sep 21, 1965	0.12	3,003,000
Slovakia	Jan 19, 1993	*	5,274,000
Slovenia	May 22, 1992	*	1,985,000
Solomon Islands	Sep 19, 1978	0.01	321,000
Somalia	Sep 20, 1960	0.01	7,497,000
South Africa	Nov 7, 1945	0.41	35,282,000
Spain	Dec 14, 1955	1.98	39,025,000
Sri Lanka	Dec 14, 1955	0.01	16,993,000
Sudan	Nov 12, 1956	0.01	25,204,000
Suriname	Dec 4, 1975	0.01	422,000
Swaziland	Sep 24, 1968	0.01	768,000
Sweden	Nov 19, 1946	1.11	8,642,000
Syrian Arab Republic	Oct 24, 1945	0.04	12,116,000
Tajikistan	Mar 2, 1992	*	5,357,000
Thailand	Dec 16, 1946	0.11	57,196,000

MEMBER STATE	ADMITTED	ASSESSMENT %	POPULATION (est.)
Togo	Sep 20, 1960	0.01	3,531,000
Trinidad & Tobago	Sep 18, 1962	0.05	1,253,000
Tunisia	Nov 12, 1956	0.03	8,180,000
Turkey	Oct 24, 1945	0.27	57,326,000
Turkmenistan	Mar 2, 1992	*	3,714,000
Uganda	Oct 25, 1962	0.01	16,583,000
Ukraine	Oct 24, 1945	1.18	51,944,000
United Arab Emirates	Dec 9, 1971	0.21	1,589,000
United Kingdom of Great Britain & Northern Ireland	Oct 24, 1945	5.02	57,411,000
United Republic of Tanzania	Dec 14, 1961	0.01	25,635,000
United States of America	Oct 24, 1945	25.00	253,887,000
Uruguay	Dec 18, 1945	0.04	3,096,000
Uzbekistan	Mar 2, 1992	*	20,708,000
Vanuatu	Sep 15, 1981	0.01	147,000
Venezuela	Nov 15, 1945	0.49	18,105,000
Viet Nam	Sep 20, 1977	0.01	66,200,000
Yemen	Sep 30, 1947	0.01	11,282,000
Yugoslavia	Oct 24, 1945	0.42	23,991,000
Zaire	Sep 20, 1960	0.01	36,672,000
Zambia	Dec 1, 1964	0.01	8,023,000
Zimbabwe	Aug 25, 1980	0.01	9,369,000

3

Achievement and Distress
since the UN Was Created

Humanity has advanced on several critical fronts in the past fifty years.

- Most nations have already won their freedom. And the prospects for self-determination have never looked brighter in the few remaining areas, particularly in South Africa and in the Middle East. In the past fifty years, the United Nations family has grown from 51 countries to 185.

- The world is safer today from the threat of nuclear holocaust. With the end of the Cold War and the conclusion of several disarmament agreements, it is difficult to recall that so many generations since the Second World War grew up with the constant fear of a sudden, unpredictable nuclear suicide.

- The record of human development during this period is unprecedented, with the developing countries setting a pace three times faster than the industrial countries did a century ago. Rising life expectancy, falling infant mortality, increasing educational attainment, and much improved nutrition are a few of the heartening indicators of this human advance.

- While nearly 70 percent of humanity survived in abysmal human conditions in 1960 (below a human development index of 0.4), only 35 percent suffered such conditions in 1992. The share of the world population enjoying fairly satisfactory human development levels (above a Human Development Index of 0.6) increased from 25 percent in 1960 to 60 percent in 1992.

- The wealth of nations has multiplied in these fifty years. Global GDP has increased sevenfold, from about $3 trillion to $22 trillion. Since the world population has more than doubled — from 2.5 billion to 5.5 billion — per capita income has more than tripled.

Reprinted with permission from the United Nations Development Programme *Human Development Report 1994* (New York, Oxford University Press).

- There have also been dramatic developments in technology. In 1927, the first transatlantic flight by Charles Lindbergh took thirty-three hours. Today, the Concorde can fly the Atlantic in about a tenth of that time. And most parts of the world are now immediately accessible by telephone, television, or fax. Computers move more than a trillion dollars around the world's financial markets every twenty-four hours.

- Human ingenuity has led to several technological innovations and breathtaking breakthroughs — from an informatics revolution to exciting space explorations, from ever-new medical frontiers to ever-greater additions to knowledge. Sometimes, human institutions have even failed to keep up with technological progress, so fast has been the pace of advance.

- Global military spending has declined significantly in the past six years, after awesome increases in the previous four decades. How intelligently this emerging peace dividend will be used is now up to policy-makers.

- Between one-half and three-quarters of the world's people live under relatively pluralistic and democratic regimes. In 1993 alone, elections were held in forty-five countries — in some for the first time.

This recapitulation of human progress is admittedly selective. But it shows that it is possible — indeed mandatory — to engineer change. Today's anxieties should not be allowed to paralyze tomorrow's initiatives. Nor can there be complacency, since a lengthening agenda of human deprivation still awaits us.

- Despite all our technological breakthroughs, we still live in a world where a fifth of the developing world's population goes hungry every night, a quarter lacks access to even a basic necessity like safe drinking water, and a third lives in a state of abject poverty — at such a margin of human existence that words simply fail to describe it.

- We also live in a world of disturbing contrasts — where so many go hungry, there is so much food to waste; where so many children do not live to enjoy their childhood, there are so many inessential weapons. Global military spending, despite a welcome decline, still equals the combined income of one-half of humanity each year. And the richest billion people command sixty times the income of the poorest billion.

- Poor nations and rich are afflicted by growing human distress — weakening social fabrics, rising crime rates, increasing threats to personal security, spreading narcotic drugs, and a growing sense of individual isolation.

- The threats to human security are no longer just personal or local or national. They are becoming global: with drugs, AIDS, terrorism, pollution, nuclear proliferation. Global poverty and environmental problems respect no national border. Their grim consequences travel the world.
- The same speed that has helped unify the world has also brought many problems to our doorsteps with devastating suddenness. Drug dealers can launder money rapidly through many countries, in a fraction of the time it takes their victims to detoxify. And terrorists operating from a remote safe haven can destroy life on a distant continent.
- The basic question of human survival on an environmentally fragile planet has gained in urgency as well. By the middle of the next century — still in the lifetimes of today's children — the world population may double and the world economy may quadruple. Food production must triple if people are to be adequately fed, but the resource base for sustainable agriculture is eroding. Energy must be provided, too, but even at today's level of use, fossil fuels threaten climatic stability. The destruction of the world's forests and the loss of biological wealth and diversity continue relentlessly.
- Several nation states are beginning to disintegrate. While the threats to national survival may emerge from several sources — ethnic, religious, political — the underlying causes are often the lack of socio-economic progress and the limited participation of people in any such progress.

Against this background of human achievement and human distress, we must seek a new concept of human security in the decades ahead. We must seek a new paradigm of sustainable human development that can satisfy the expanding frontiers of this human security. We must seek a new framework of development cooperation that brings humanity together through a more equitable sharing of global economic opportunities and responsibilities. And we must seek a new role for the United Nations so that it can begin to meet humanity's agenda not only for peace but also for development.

4

Toward the Next Fifty Years

Richard Butler

President Woodrow Wilson, at the end of a terrible, terrible world war, announced his fourteen principles that he hoped would guide the subsequent conduct of international relations and bring about a system in which war would be outlawed. That was in 1918. What he had in mind was the creation of a world organization that was the League of Nations. But it ran into difficulties that, interestingly, are not very different from the difficulties that we are facing at the end of the Cold War.

Those difficulties included the second act of what I like to call the "wars of European tribalism" (World Wars I and II). At the end of that disastrous second act, in May of 1945, the world's leaders met again to pick up the broken threads of world unity.

For six weeks, in the period May–June 1945, the then forty-six countries that constituted the free world community met in San Francisco, and on June 24, 1945, signed a document called the Charter of the United Nations, which then entered into force on October 24, 1945. And it is that date, October 1945, that compels us and inspires us to celebrate the fiftieth anniversary of the United Nations.

But the UN is facing problems that are the consequences of the end of a conflict (in this case not a hot war but a cold war), and problems of economy, social development, and justice among people. I think we've got every reason for pride and satisfaction that our organization, unlike the League of Nations, will have made it to a half century. It has every prospect of continuing to live, and to live strongly, in the future. But let us not just have the fiftieth anniversary only as a cause for pride and celebration. Let us seize it as an opportunity for renewal.

I'd like to talk about the subjects that we can address nationally and in-

This essay is adapted from an address to the United Nations Association of the USA in January 1994 by His Excellency Richard Butler, Permanent Representative of Australia to the UN and chair of the United Nations 50th Anniversary Committee.

ternationally in that process of renewal. By referring to the Preamble of the Charter of the United Nations, you will see a coequal set of four major objectives of the world community. The first of them is peace, the second is equality, the third is justice, and the fourth is development.

It seems to me that we must renew our organization in a way that will make it capable of addressing all of those challenges if it is to survive and to prosper in its second fifty years. If it does not, it will have the support of people around the world. The removal of the threat of nuclear destruction, the removal of conflict between superpowers, has brought to the top of our agenda the pressing non-military and human concerns that people face around the world today. They are concerns about a decent standard of living, a job, a predictable pattern of public health, concerns of women, concerns of infant mortality, and so on.

It is very clear to me, as a contemporary practitioner at the United Nations today, that if we will fail to address those issues, we do so at our peril. The UN cannot simply become a house that makes peace through peacemaking. If it is to stand, it must stand on all of its four legs in the future, not just the leg called peace, but also the three called equality, justice, and development.

We hear voices being raised, saying in a rather negative and pessimistic fashion that the UN is in trouble, that it's not fulfilling the aims and expectations held of it by so many people. Be careful of criticism of the United Nations that places the blame in the wrong place. The principles in the charter are sound. The will of the international community to allow it to do its job is pretty sound. Very often, criticism is misplaced, because it rests on a misperception of what the United Nations is and what it is able to do under its charter.

How many of our young people today know that the fabric of modern international society is a fabric designed, built, and managed by the United Nations? Do our young people know that when you post a letter today anywhere in the world, it goes there under UN rules? Do they know that all ships that sail the seas sail under UN rules? Do they know that all aircraft flying the world skies fly under UN rules; that the radio waves that are allocated to broadcasters are allocated under UN rules; that faxes and telegrams and satellite links are allocated under UN rules? Do they know that smallpox was eliminated by the World Health Organization? Why is it that in many countries of the world children no longer are put to work below age? Because of the rules of the International Labor Organization. My point is this, that while we fought the Cold War and got stultified in that awful situation, the UN didn't sleep.

The UN, from 1945 to now, has built a fabric of international law, practice, habit, cooperation, and regulation that constitutes modern society in the technological age.

There is a process of adult education required, too, directed toward adjusting perceptions of what people can reasonably expect of the UN, what its charter and role is, and what we might encourage it and support it to do in the future. It's critical, because of the impact that these perceptions have on funding for the UN, through the Congresses and the Parliaments.

And then, of course, celebration. How wonderful it will be if, in 1995, we can see acts of celebration in countries around the world, from the small poster exhibitions in little schools up to the great opera houses and symphony halls of the world. Good, honest celebration of a truly important human achievement, joined to the immense talent and skill that we have in the artistic and cultural communities.

What will those of us who represent our governments do? A drafting group open to all member states of the UN is creating the Declaration of the General Assembly of the United Nations of 1995. That will be on the table on October 24, 1995. It will pick up the charter and say, "These purposes and these principles were right in 1945 and they are right today." But the challenges to peace, equality, justice, and development are different today from what they were then. So we need a road map by which to drive our charter.

We need to give greater emphasis to the environment than we did in 1945. We need to give greater emphasis to the rights of women than we did in 1945. We need to spread the message and the law on human rights to a greater extent than we did in 1945. We need to address non-military threats to security in a way that we never have done before. We need to accept that more people in this world today are threatened by poverty than they are by war. Likewise, more people are threatened by the illicit trade in arms and narcotic drugs than by war.

If we want peace, equality, justice, and development in the world, then all of the facilities of the United Nations, including the Security Council, should be more sharply directed to non-military threats to security than they have been in the past. It's that kind of road map that I hope we will draw. It will sit alongside the charter, and will constitute the main political outcome of the fiftieth anniversary.

We need a more highly textured definition of what constitutes security. We need to recognize that for most people in the world, their basic goal is to have a decent standard of living for themselves and their children and to enjoy it in a framework of peace. The United Nations is uniquely able to deliver those things. Its fiftieth birthday is an opportunity that we must seize.

We cannot do what we need to have done solely by the actions of governments. I have not the slightest doubt that we will achieve these objectives only through the commitment of non-governmental organizations; that we would never have made the strides we have made in disarmament without non-governmental pressure. The same is true with regard to the environment. And the same will be true of the fiftieth anniversary of the UN. I ask for your cooperation, because we cannot do it alone.

Part Two

THE ISSUES

WE THE PEOPLES OF THE UNITED NATIONS DETERMINED

- to save succeeding generations from the scourge of war ...

AND FOR THESE ENDS

- to practice tolerance and live together in peace with one another as good neighbors, and
- to unite our strength to maintain international peace and security, and
- to ensure, by acceptance of principles and the institution of meth-ods, that armed force shall not be used, save in the common interest, and ...

HAVE RESOLVED TO COMBINE OUR EFFORTS TO ACCOMPLISH THESE AIMS ...

—from the Preamble to the Charter of the United Nations

•

He shall judge between many peoples, and shall arbitrate between strong nations far away; they shall beat their swords into plowshares, and their spears into pruning hooks; nation shall not lift up sword against nation, neither shall they learn war any more; but they shall all sit under their own vines and under their own fig trees, and no one shall make them afraid; for the mouth of the Lord of hosts has spoken.

—Micah 4:3–4

5

Building the Conditions for Peace:
Beyond the Blue Helmets

Bonnie M. Greene

Imagine your life without the United Nations. For most of us, it would be hard to describe the difference. At least that's what I thought, until the day my daughters and I heard on the radio the voice of one of the Canadians who witnessed the first dismantling of a nuclear warhead in the former USSR. We cried. For forty-five years (my entire life), the major powers had been building one nuclear weapon after another, preparing to go to war. Finally, through a formal agreement, the two major nuclear powers agreed to take one step back from the brink of a war into which we would all have been drawn. We all breathed a sigh of relief.

No one will ever know for certain whether that small step backward could have been achieved without the UN. Had the UN not existed, however, it would have been exceedingly difficult for governments to reach important agreements in the fields of peacekeeping, arms control, and disarmament. Surely some credit must go to the UN for keeping wars between states to a minimum, during a time when our capacity to kill our enemies — and everyone living near them — grew beyond imagination.

No one would claim that the UN has put an end to war. Major nuclear weapons systems are still in place. Worse, more people are dying in wars today than at any time during my lifetime. They are dying in the "other" wars — the thirty-eight full-blown civil wars in countries that we in the United States and Canada could scarcely see, until the missiles began to move out of our line of vision.

Does the UN have anything to offer the millions of people for whom there

DR. BONNIE GREENE is the director of the Office of Church in Society of the United Church of Canada. She serves on the International Affairs Committee and the Foreign Policy Review Steering Committee of the Canadian Council of Churches, and on the Executive Committee of Project Ploughshares, a leading Canadian peace organization established by the Canadian churches. She serves on the Churches' Human Rights Program in the CSCE, a program of the U.S., Canadian, and European councils of churches.

have been virtually no steps back from the brink of conventional war? At the moment, not really. And why is that? The answer lies partly with the original members of the UN and the way in which they translated the initial world vision into the real organization. It also lies in the changed face of war-making in the 1990s.

The UN: A Talking Table

Not everyone who witnessed the use of nuclear weapons in Hiroshima and Nagasaki understood what it meant for world order. To many it looked like a confirmation of the old adage about "carrying a very big stick" if you want to be safe. Some people, though, realized that the invention of nuclear weapons meant that the world must wean itself from trying to solve conflicts by military means.

Further, the introduction of the bomb turned several nations into "global warriors." Their ability to disrupt human life and to command power on a world scale rested on the size of their nuclear "big sticks." The only possibility for the survival of the planet, therefore, was to create a talking table, with a place set for the representatives of every nation — even those who behaved like enemies. The hosts would do everything in their power to keep the global warriors (and all the other leaders) talking, until they discovered common interests. The hope was that over time they might gain enough confidence in the other people at the table to set their fears aside. Eventually, they might even give up warfare as a means of dealing with enemies.

The leaders called this talking table the United Nations. One condition of membership was that all guests had to leave their weapons at the door. But, unfortunately, the global warriors insisted on a parallel process. Back home, their scientists and generals prepared for battle at a moment's notice — just in case talking didn't work. The miracle is that for fifty years the UN has kept the warriors talking and persuaded the nuclear powers to restrain themselves from using every weapon at their disposal.

Back in 1945, it seemed obvious that the world must never again take up weapons, that the member nations must put war behind them once and for all. They must evolve until they could rely on diplomacy and on promises made and kept as the most effective way to deal with the inevitable differences that would arise. The goal of creating a kind of global federation became the driving vision for idealists involved in the UN in the early days. Virtually every nation came to the UN table. States made verbal commitments to seek political and diplomatic solutions to conflict, to respect the borders of every state (no invasions), and to keep their word that they would not use state power to kill their own people. The idealistic vision soon faded as the UN found itself occupied with practical and political challenges that were complicated both by the structure of the UN and by the kinds of crises that first challenged the fledgling organization during the 1950s.

The UN created a senior committee whose members — the major nuclear weapons states — became the permanent members of the Security Council. The United Kingdom, China, France, the former Soviet Union, and the United States were allowed to create a separate table and were given the power to make the most important decisions. All the countries affected by their decisions could watch the debates in the UN and the process outside the UN, but they could not vote or even engage in the debate, except when they were allowed to take their turn sitting at the Security Council table for a brief time.

Given the way the Security Council was set up, it isn't very surprising that the UN failed to close down the parallel process of war preparation. It did little to restrain scientists, technologists, and manufacturers from harnessing the best minds and resources they could muster to prepare the most terrifying arsenals money and brains could create.

The UN became a "talking shop" — exactly what its founders had intended — in order that political consensus would replace the use of force to settle disputes. It was a dangerous gamble. Though building consensus is an excellent way to spread a sense of ownership, it was a political process that was quickly outstripped by developments in military technology. When all the countries affected by a possible war sat down to the same table, they were not all equals. The countries that most endangered others — the ones that were most likely to go to war — could drag their feet on a consensus for a very long time, while their people at home prepared to destroy everyone else. And that is exactly what happened.

The UN's detractors said, "The UN is only a debating society. It is useless in dealing with serious conflict." The implication was that talking was not enough. Critics offered several conflicting solutions: Give the UN more resources. Admit the UN isn't worth what it costs, and abolish it. Create a UN army. Put the strongest in charge (usually the U.S.). Admit what we all know: "Unless the United States agrees, we won't have world peace."

In the competitive, result-driven culture of the United States and Canada, these arguments appealed to many people. But, by design, the UN is the kind of organization that appears to fail, because in the world of peacemaking success is a non-event. It is a war that doesn't happen, a missile that rusts out before it is used, and enemies lowering their clenched fists to shake hands.

When it works, the UN's success in the security field emphasizes peacemaking as a process rather than the result-driven goal of victory. It attracts little news coverage. It advances day-by-day in small increments. The results are hard to measure, especially if the players at the table change positions, as they often do in Western democracies.

For many of us, the UN's success is seldom visible. And indeed, after fifty years, the UN has failed to bring an end to war. For years the arms race and conflicts between states have robbed people and the environment of huge quantities of resources that might have been used to fight the underlying causes of social tensions and war in the first place. In its recent peacekeeping efforts in Bosnia and Somalia, the UN has been called an occupying army by the very people that peacekeepers were sent to protect.

On the other hand, the UN surely deserves some credit for reducing the number of wars between states. Nuclear war between the United States and the USSR never happened — despite the most elaborate and costly preparations for war in the history of civilization! And despite the opinion of some Bosnians and Somalis, the UN's ability to launch peacekeeping missions represents a fragile but respected resource for keeping conflict under control once peace breaks down.

The Churches' Role in the UN

It is no accident that the United Nations and the World Council of Churches (WCC) were created at roughly the same time, that they have major offices near each other in Geneva, and that the ecumenical Church Center for the UN is across the street from the UN headquarters in New York City. From its inception, the World Council of Churches has helped focus the resources of the churches on supporting the development of certain international agreements that have become the standard code of ethics for the global community — especially in the area of human rights, development, and peace.

Some people say that the churches took this action because they yearned for power and status. That might have been a motivation for a few, but most were simply people looking for ways to hasten "the healing of the nations." The UN was an arena for practical discipleship in the service of God and neighbor. Three fundamental issues of faith drove church people to invest so much in the UN.

First, at the end of World War II, a handful of mainstream church leaders realized that traditional ethical thinking by Christians was not going to work in the interests of all of humanity in the age of nuclear weapons. In fact, our traditional thinking was at risk of being used by some political leaders to justify unthinkable devastation. For centuries, Christian thinkers had been assisting kings, and later nation states, in working out such questions as these: Under what circumstances is the king, or the state, morally justified in going to war with another king or state? What rules must the king follow to avoid harming innocent people in the process, especially civilians and members of non-enemy states? How should the victorious king treat the defeated people and their leaders? The concept of a "just war" had evolved from the time that the early Christians lived under Roman occupation.

The issue emerged only gradually in the early church. Followers of Jesus were the fiercer pacifists until roughly 300 c.e., partly because the Roman Empire did not trust Christians in military roles, believing they might put loyalty to God and Jesus before duty to the emperor. Eventually, though, the Christian community began to develop its own thinking about the duties it owed to other people. Christians gradually expanded their understanding of Jesus' command to love God, love one's neighbor, and love oneself. They had originally interpreted love as doing good for others and not doing harm, which was pretty straightforward. The problem arose when they saw people around them harming other people: they concluded that Christians had a duty to prevent such harm or evil.

Eventually, the early Christians concluded that followers of Christ were obliged to do all they could to remove evil or harm. Therefore, loving God and neighbor meant they had to share responsibility for looking after the interests of the weakest. When invading armies began to weaken the Roman Empire, making life unstable, the issue of Christian discipleship shifted ground: What means can we use to prevent harm to others? Once Christians decided that they could express love by using lethal military force to defend others, the stage was set for centuries of debate. From that time until Hiroshima-Nagasaki, much of the church's energy — apart from the small historic peace churches — was devoted to working out rules for the use of force as a means of loving God and loving one's neighbor.

It took just one bomb to make it crystal clear that the rules worked out over sixteen centuries had been outstripped by the technology of war available to us. Nuclear weapons ignored boundaries between states and threatened all people, not just the "enemy." Having at their command the ability to destroy all human life gave to people a power that should belong only to God, according to Christian thinkers. They began trying to build an ethical consensus that no matter what we might feel about our enemies, there were some kinds of weapons we must never allow ourselves to use. The UN became the place where a political consensus could be built among people no matter what their cultural or political starting point.

The second major faith issue that drove church visionaries to support the UN was the recognition that the world could not rely on people everywhere accepting a supreme and universal moral authority to offer guidance in resisting nuclear war and building a global "society." For centuries people had been accustomed to moral reasoning about the kind of war that was limited both by the kinds of weapons that states could bring to their cause and by the difficulties of transporting armies over long distances. By the 1950s, twentieth-century inventions in weapons and travel had made warfare a long-distance activity.

Therefore it gradually became clear that politicians could no longer use real experience with the enemy to guide political decisions about going to war or resolving the conflict. With a long-distance enemy, they couldn't assume that their people and the enemy's people shared the same belief system. Building trust and confidence with distant enemies became a risky business. (Think of the years during which Westerners heard about "the godless Soviets" and vice versa.) In the age of nuclear weapons, global decision-makers were certain to come to the UN table with conflicting sources of moral authority. For the sake of humanity, the major faith communities of the world — Jewish, Christian, Muslim, Buddhist, and others — needed to draw on their own best traditions to offer people a common moral ground for dealing with enemies in a very dangerous world. In the 1940s and 1950s the World Council of Churches was an important mechanism for bringing together Christians from every part of the globe for this delicate task.

A third faith issue that brought Christians to the UN in the 1940s and 1950s was the Holocaust. The churches that helped form the WCC had been horrified by the Holocaust and the meaning it had for minorities of every kind. It was unthinkable that the Holocaust had happened at all, but it was even more unthinkable that some had justified it on grounds of Christian faith. One group of people had been able to designate another group of people as disposable, in the name of God. It was a fundamental affront to the teaching of Jesus about identity with God in Christ and therefore solidarity with all human beings.

For these and other reasons, church leaders of the 1940s and 1950s put a great deal of energy into the United Nations, both its vision and its practice. On the practical side, it took time and courage on the part of many Christians to make that vision concrete and practical in their own lives. Europeans tell a wonderful story of how the vision spread from a few leaders to many people in the churches on both sides of the Cold War. The political division of Europe into enemy and ally camps meant that church workers found themselves almost powerless in dealing with people's very practical pastoral needs getting visas to visit the "enemy" side for a funeral or consoling families permanently separated by arbitrary political and ideological divisions.

Finally, some of the church people decided that the division of the people of God was an insult to the gospel taught by Jesus. They simply said: "We refuse to live as enemies of one another." A few people from both sides of the East-West divide got together to talk. They had to meet on a ship in international waters because of visa restrictions. For them, that was the beginning of the end of the Cold War. They disarmed their hearts and minds and began to thaw the Cold War from below, while their politicians shouted rhetoric at one another and stockpiled weapons.

Containing War between States: The First Challenge for the UN

When the UN was created, political leaders were preoccupied with the security of those nation states that remained after the ceasefire. While many states sent their people to the UN table to talk, they spent much more of their time organizing themselves into military alliances such as the North Atlantic Treaty Organization (NATO) and the Warsaw Treaty Organization (WTO). As long as other states looked like enemies that might invade their territory, most states could find public support for investing their resources in new weapons systems, in military alliances, and in building up political will to resist the enemy. Politicians had only to say, "If you want peace, prepare for war," and a sea of heads would nod. Federal budgets, industrial planning, and even entire towns became part of the effort to prepare for war, should political leaders decide the time had come.

Countries that wanted to take a different approach committed a great deal of energy to containing or preventing war. At the UN, they pressed for arms control treaties, agreements on troop placements, banning chemical and biological weapons, nuclear non-proliferation treaties, and so on.

Preventing war was not enough. They also had to turn their minds to *stopping* war or keeping a war in a fairly small space from getting bigger. After all, a small war could easily become the "war to end all wars," if a nuclear state stepped in. If the talking at the UN table was unable to prevent war, the UN would need some other resource to confine war in its early stages. Otherwise, the debates would appear to be empty rhetoric and the UN would lose credibility. One solution emerged when the Suez crisis developed. To prevent the conflict from escalating, the UN decided to create a team of international security guards available to protect a peace process.

In the early days, UN peacekeepers were military people sent to stand between parties to a conflict. Their job was to supervise a truce or a ceasefire or to ensure that a skirmish was not able to scuttle diplomatic talks aimed at a permanent peace. In such situations, the UN peacekeepers had a limited mandate. In some cases, they were also asked to take on tasks that were aimed at helping civilians cope with the chaos and danger war posed for them; for example:

- delivering humanitarian aid to civilians (blankets, food, water, emergency medicine);
- escorting refugees and arranging for their care while displaced;
- guarding basic services, such as power and water systems, if possible;
- monitoring the treatment of prisoners of war.

To accomplish this, the peacekeepers were backed up by a team of global "social workers" who worked alongside them. They were drawn from the humanitarian side of the UN's operation, such as the High Commission for Refugees, and from the International Committee of the Red Cross and Red Crescent. The peacekeepers and the "social workers" were usually people of deep courage and humanitarian commitment, but increasingly they were shorthanded and dreadfully overworked.

Over time, as the Security Council made decisions about specific crises, it added new tasks to the job descriptions of its peacekeepers. For example, the UN can send unarmed peacekeepers into a country to monitor human rights violations or even to stand guard while a new democratic government tries to get on its feet, as in Namibia.

In the post-Cold War period, wars have been primarily between groups of people within states, or civil wars, or between the supporters of rival political leaders for control of the government, as in Somalia. The UN has turned more and more often to its peacekeepers as a resource both for containing small civil wars and for preventing social conflict from breaking down to war. Unfortunately, the UN was never designed, mandated, or equipped to deal with such conflicts. Therefore, it has been nearly impossible to reach a timely consensus on exactly what it may do to address a crisis like the Rwanda war of 1994.

Peacekeeping at the Crossroads

Peacekeeping is being attacked openly for its failures in the wars that have erupted since 1989. The criticisms are usually these:

- The goals are not clear.
- The UN is being arbitrary, partisan, or racist when it decides which conflicts it asks peacekeepers to take on.
- UN peacekeeping has become a smokescreen for American domination of the world.
- The UN turns a blind eye to conflicts that are in the interests of one of the permanent members of the Security Council — Russia in Chechnya, for example.
- The people who serve on UN missions are neither trained nor equipped to deal with the well-armed soldiers they have to meet in the field.

- The missions create markets for the war entrepreneurs who open shop in all war zones, especially those in organized crime and the arms trade.
- And finally, peacekeepers are being sent into situations where peace has broken down so completely that nothing can be done to protect the local people unless the UN decides to *enforce* peace by using lethal military force itself.

These attacks are coming at a time when the UN is being called on for more and more peacekeeping activity. The UN actually set up nearly as many new peacekeeping operations in the first half of the 1990s as it did in the previous forty years. The strain is beginning to show. The Security Council decides to send out the peacekeepers without being sure it has the money or the people to carry out the operation. It is far behind in paying its peacekeeping bills, and it owes large amounts of money to the countries that contribute people and other resources to its missions. Security Council operations are not well coordinated with the work of its humanitarian organizations. Therefore, the UN has little ability to tap the crucial resources for stopping a war that lie within the country itself. Poorly planned operations like those in Somalia and Bosnia-Herzegovina have hurt the UN's credibility, even with the civilians it was hoping to protect.

The UN's failures in bringing civil wars to an end should surprise no one. It exists to protect states — especially weak states — from being attacked by other states. It has the right to intervene in civil wars only because it has an obligation to local people to set up its humanitarian operations in a war zone when they can't get water, medicine, food, or a safe place to sleep at night. It keeps that right only if it moves slowly in building consensus. The UN — like every other institution — has virtually no experience to draw on when it tries to stop a civil war. Yet the world continues to turn to it for action.

Post-Cold War Conflict at a Glance

The UN issued a sobering study on the different qualities of wars before and after the Cold War (*Rebuilding Wartorn Societies*, UN Research Institute for Social Development, Geneva, September 1993). In 1994, there were eighty-five conflicts under way in our world. Thirty-eight were "wars" (conflicts where military forces were involved and at least a thousand people died) in the Third World and the former Second World. Thirteen were in Africa; eleven in central Asia.

These wars were waged with weapons that were designed and exported worldwide primarily by the United States, Russia, France, the United Kingdom, China, India, Afghanistan, Brazil, and Saudi Arabia. The military conflicts of the 1990s were between groups of people within countries,

UN Peacekeeping Operations

UNTSO: UN Truce Supervision Organization in Israel and Syria, Israel and Lebanon, Israel and Egypt June 1948 to present

UNMOGIP: UN Military Observer Group in India and Pakistan January 1949 to present

UNEF I: First UN Emergency Force in Egypt and Israel November 1956–June 1967

UNOGIL: UN Observation Group in Lebanon June 1958–December 1958

ONUC: UN Operation in the Congo July 1960–June 1964

UNSF: UN Security Force in West New Guinea (West Irian) October 1962–April 1963

UNYOM: UN Yemen Observation Mission July 1963–September 1964

UNFICYP: UN Peacekeeping Force in Cyprus March 1964 to present

DOMREP: Mission of the Representative of the Secretary General in the Dominican Republic May 1965–October 1966

UNIPOM: UN India-Pakistan Observation Mission September 1965–March 1966

UNEF II: Second UN Emergency Force in Israel and Egypt, Israel and Syria October 1973–July 1979

UNDOF: UN Disengagement Observer Force in Israel and Egypt, Israel and Syria June 1974 to present

UNIFIL: UN Interim Force in Lebanon March 1978 to present

UNGOMAP: UN Good Offices Mission in Afghanistan & Pakistan April 1988–March 1990

UNIIMOG: UN Iran-Iraq Military Observer Group August 1988–February 1991

UNAVEM I: UN Angola Verification Mission I January 1989–June 1991

UNTAG: UN Transition Assistance Group in Namibia April 1989–March 1990

ONUCA: UN Observer Group in Central America November 1989–January 1992

UNIKOM: UN Iraq-Kuwait Observation Mission April 1991 to present

UNAVEM II: UN Angola Verification Mission II June 1991 to 1994

ONUSAL: UN Observer Mission in El Salvador July 1991 to present

MINURSO: UN Mission for the Referendum in Western Sahara September 1991 to present

UNAMIC: UN Advance Mission in Cambodia October 1991–March 1992

UNPROFOR: UN Protection Force in Bosnia-Herzegovina, Croatia, the Federal Republic of Yugoslavia, the former Yugoslav Republic of Macedonia March 1992 to present

UNTAC: UN Transitional Authority in Cambodia March 1992–September 1993

UNOSOM I: UN Operation in Somalia I April 1992–April 1993

ONUMOZ: UN Operation in Mozambique December 1992 to 1995

UNOSOM II: UN Operation in Somalia II May 1993 to present

UNOMUR: UN Observer Mission in Uganda-Rwanda June 1993 to present

UNOMIG: UN Observer Mission in Georgia August 1993 to present

UNOMIL: UN Observer Mission in Liberia September 1993 to present

UNMIH: UN Mission in Haiti September 1993 to present

UNAMIR: UN Assistance Mission for Rwanda October 1993 to present

UNASOG: UN Aouzou Strip Observer Group in Chad and Libya May 1994–June 1994

[As a result of the peace treaty of November 1994, Angola became the newest UN peacekeeping operation.]

UN Peacekeeping Operations

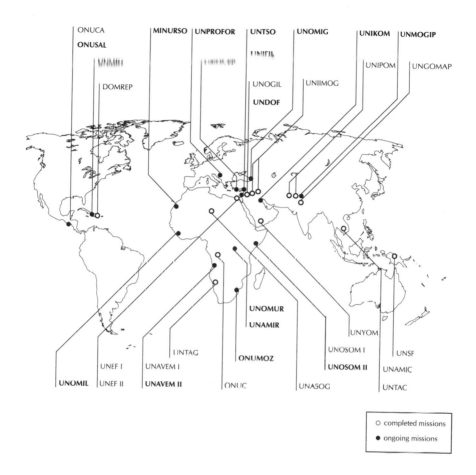

ONUCA
ONUSAL
UNAVEM
DOMREP
MINURSO
UNPROFOR
UNTSO
UNIFIL
UNOGIL
UNDOF
UNOMIG
UNIIMOG
UNIKOM
UNIPOM
UNMOGIP
UNGOMAP

UNOMUR
UNAMIR
ONUMOZ
UNYOM
UNOSOM I
UNOSOM II
UNSF
UNAMIC
UNTAG
UNAVEM I
UNEF I
UNOMIL
UNEF II
UNAVEM II
ONUC
UNASOG
UNTAC

○ completed missions
● ongoing missions

especially those countries unable to meet the security needs of all their people.

According to the UN, today's internal wars last longer than wars between nations. They cause the collapse of governments. They kill few soldiers but massacre hundreds of thousands of civilians. They create millions of displaced people. (One out of every 130 people on the face of the earth is presently displaced by war.) These wars swamp the economic and social capabilities of neighboring countries. They destroy the delicate fabric of entire societies, turning whole populations into victims — maimed, orphaned, or made "stateless" through sieges and "ethnic cleansing."

Civil wars destroy the psyche of an entire society, because they often rely on atrocities rather than mass bombing to make people submit — atrocities such as public rape, mutilation, and torture. They turn teenagers and children into soldiers who are counseled by their elders to kill rather than to restrain their instincts for violence. They hire unemployed soldiers from other countries as mercenaries. Local unemployed people often find themselves making a living as members of death squads and militia run by warlords.

These are not video game wars, run by a handful of people with their fingers on the buttons and the enemy's buildings for targets. They are far more chaotic than that. In these wars, people cannot calculate their chances for survival based on where they live because there are thousands of "fronts" in a civil war, and the enemy may be the farmer who lives across the road.

How on earth did this happen? It was very simple really. While the UN tried to build the habits of cooperation among entire nations, few resources were invested in building the habits of cooperation and human rights among peoples within nations — especially those who lived in the command systems of the former Soviet-dominated countries and some parts of Africa. The member states also dragged their feet so much that they gave some people the chance to fill a market niche for high-tech and powerful conventional weapons (guns, land mines, helicopters, tanks, surface-to-air missiles, combat aircraft, self-propelled guns, etc.).

For the moderately upscale market, technology and science have helped some business people find ingenious ways to supply the market demand. One new conventional weapon uses laser beams instead of bullets. Its effect is to blind, rather than kill, the enemy. Still other weapons have been redesigned to make them cheap, portable, and small enough to hide under the family bed. (Beirut was flooded with weapons of this sort during the Lebanese war.)

For the unhappy citizens of very poor countries, other entrepreneurs used the time to set up the equivalent of a discount mall for low-income warriors. They even created a "gently used" department for countries that don't mind taking another country's hand-me-down weapons.

The Challenges of Building and Keeping Peace

Ambassador Jan Eliasson, former UN Under-Secretary-General for Humanitarian Affairs, has pointed out that the UN, as it was originally set up, is nearly powerless to protect men, women, and children who are under fire, trapped in a siege, or forcibly displaced in ethnic cleansing. No matter how deep the sense of moral obligation, no outside party — not even the Blue Helmets — can stop a civil war unless the people involved in the war want to stop fighting.

One of the terrible lessons of the post-Cold War period is that amassing enough power to persuade leaders of our own countries to give up preparations for nuclear war in Europe was relatively easy. When it comes to stopping other people's wars, our power is far less than we imagine. Major-General Lewis MacKenzie put it succinctly just before he completed his term as head of the UN operation in Bosnia-Herzegovina: "If I could convince both sides to stop killing their own people for CNN [Cable News Network], perhaps we could have a ceasefire."

Defense specialists say the world urgently needs to replace a "security doctrine" based on military force with a comprehensive approach that would concentrate on political and economic issues in conflicts, such as sustainable development and humanitarian assistance, and psycho-sociological issues such as "enemy images," racial and ethnic hatred, and the use of religion to justify killing.

A new kind of peacekeeping has begun to emerge in the UN, described by Boutros Boutros-Ghali in *An Agenda for Peace* as "peace operations." Sending peacekeepers into a country to create "safe havens" or to stand guard around the perimeter of a war zone to prevent the war from spreading represent a dangerous path both for the peacekeepers and for the UN, not to mention the civilians caught in the middle.

Even military leaders have begun to press the UN for more investment in one of Boutros-Ghali's more idealistic suggestions: preventive diplomacy. The people caught in war zones deserve a "peace race" on a scale at least as great as the efforts we devoted to preventing nuclear war in our own part of the world. Perhaps it is time to equip ourselves collectively for the more difficult job of building peaceful relationships between peoples who regard each other as enemies and to invest in building the conditions in which peace can flourish, given the will in the hearts of the people.

Building a Support System for Peace

Despite the terrible human suffering in today's wars, one thing has not been tried: the non-military option on a scale equivalent to the war-making capacity of today's warlords. However, the UN can never hope to have the staff or the organization to do that job by itself on behalf of the entire world. Based on its experience with non-governmental organizations in delivering humanitarian aid in war zones, the UN has pointed out that the internal wars of the 1990s require the resources of both governments and non-governmental organizations. The idea is sometimes called "citizen diplomacy" or "Track II diplomacy" — Track I diplomacy being the work of governments.

John Paul Lederach and Gerald Shenk, Mennonite practitioners of international conflict resolution and professors in Mennonite colleges in the United States, say that the "nature of current clashes is so defined by fear, hatred, prejudice, and racism, that tools for healing and recovery will have to come from circles much broader than traditional diplomacy and negotiations. They must address emotional, perceptive, psychological, and spiritual dimensions and the core of well-being, both for individuals and for whole populations" (Gerald Shenk, *God with Us? The Roles of Religion in Conflicts in the Former Yugoslavia* [Uppsala, Sweden: Life and Peace Institute, 1993]).

Based on his experience in Central America, Africa, and Eastern Europe, Lederach says that the wars we face today require "an infrastructure of peace" that offers "an entirely new framework of international intervention." Present interventions usually depend on peace talks between presidents of countries, with UN mediators or other diplomats urging the process along. Meanwhile, war rages on. Blue Helmets and aid workers provide humanitarian aid or transport out of the area when they can. Often, NGOs and churches try to build a culture of peace at the grassroots level by investing people and resources in development projects, human rights work, education, and fragile peace campaigns. But virtually no one attends to the middle range of the institutions in which people carry out their most important activities — churches, schools and universities, cultural and professional organizations. Most of these institutions stay in place during wars, but seldom are drawn into the peace-building process. There is no effort to use the institutions to build a culture of peace that can be sustained long after the negotiators have gone home and the local projects have been completed.

This approach to peace-building rests on the belief that the most significant part of the peace-building constituency is located inside the war zone. That peace constituency exists wherever men and women find the moral courage to disarm their own hearts and psyches and create tables for sitting down with their enemies. In the new world of civil war, those are the negotiating tables that count most.

The role for churches and peace groups outside the war zone is to provide an international support system — a sustaining scaffolding — to people inside the war zone as they rebuild relationships between people who have done unspeakable things to each other and as they reweave the horribly shredded social fabrics of their societies. The occasional team visit is not enough. In a recent study done in Sri Lanka, for example, peace organizations reported that they had been visited by more than 130 different teams of people from other countries. Few developed a continuing relationship of support; fewer still returned and none distributed their reports to the Sri Lankan peace groups. Sri Lankans found that they needed more sustained support if they were to build relations between the Tamils and the Sinhalese. Lederach says we need to develop approaches that are sustained, persistent, and coordinated.

Examples of this approach have developed here and there. In the Horn of Africa, an international resource group is supporting Ethiopians and Eritreans who are creating the plan for demilitarizing the region. The resource group includes former African diplomats, peace researchers from countries such as Sweden and Canada, and former UN military leaders.

In southern Hungary, a small organization runs retreats where Muslims and Catholics from Croatian villages can meet to rebuild the relationships that will allow them to return to their towns and re-establish a multicultural life. The outside supporters come from the Netherlands and other countries. Their role is to invite the guests to a common table and create the conditions where people can heal the psycho-social wounds that war has created.

For churches in North America, this approach to peace-building is both an opportunity and a challenge to our customary ways. As churches outside today's war zones, they can rise above the partisan loyalties. They have information, finances, human resources, and psychological space that churches in the war zones may temporarily lack. They can offer energy and persistence that, over time, may help overcome resistance to action for peace.

On the other hand, churches sometimes find themselves drawn into supporting the church of their own denomination and possibly legitimizing the war rather than enhancing the peace effort. Many churches in North America are accustomed to making public statements, calling on governments to take a particular action for peace. But relying on governments and the UN to discharge our moral obligations to men and women caught up in today's wars will not be enough to build the peace race that John Paul Lederach is talking about. Finally, today's wars will challenge many churches to find practical ways of collaborating not only with Christians but also with Muslims, Hindus, and other faith communities that make up the majority in the civil wars of the post-Cold War era.

From Peacekeeping to Peace-building

The UN created an important resource when it invented peacekeeping and recruited men and women to stand guard while diplomats went about the work of resolving conflict. However, because we do not yet have the practical tools for building social peace within some individual states, we are putting peacekeeping missions at risk when we rely on peacekeeping for conflicts where they cannot possibly work. The heavy costs and the failures of Somalia and Bosnia-Herzegovina are driving some countries to say that they will have to stand back when the UN calls for new peacekeeping operations.

Peacekeeping missions have played a crucial role in protecting the lives of hundreds of thousands of people caught in ghastly wars. Nevertheless, saving lives is not a sufficient accomplishment in a civil war. Whole communities have to be put back together. Refugees have to find a way to re-establish themselves and get on with their lives. Soldiers have to develop other skills and find new jobs.

The UN desperately needs additional tools to help the world manage crises politically — and the earlier the better. "Peace-building" describes all the things we do to create the conditions in which peace can flourish because people feel secure. "Peace-building" includes monitoring human rights, promoting development, establishing the habits of mind and spirit for democratic living, and nurturing the social organizations of civil society through which people of different perspectives come to know and trust one another enough to avoid going to battle. Churches have invested in this kind of work for a very long time. It is needed today in far greater quantities and with greater coordination than ever before in human history.

Has the UN failed the visionaries who founded it? Of course it has; all of us have. But the UN also has succeeded. It has acted as a moral force in a dangerous time. It has created platforms where people of compassion and commitment have been able to work for justice and peace in the name of human decency. In the years ahead, it will need every resource people of good will can contribute to the project of building a sustainable peace, not just between nations but between peoples.

WHEREAS recognition of the inherent dignity of the equal and inalienable rights of all members of the human family is the foundation of freedom, justice and peace in the world, . . .

Now, THEREFORE, the General Assembly proclaims this Universal Declaration of Human Rights as a common standard of achievement for all peoples and all nations . . .

— from the Preamble to the Universal Declaration of Human Rights

•

Finally, all of you, have unity of spirit, sympathy, love for one another, a tender heart, and a humble mind. Do not repay evil for evil or abuse for abuse; but, on the contrary, repay with a blessing. It is for this that you were called — that you might inherit a blessing. For "Those who desire life and desire to see good days, let them keep their tongues from evil and their lips from speaking deceit; let them turn away from evil and do good; let them seek peace and pursue it."

— 1 Peter 3:8–11

6

Human Rights Is Everybody's Business

Bob Scott

The United Nations World Conference on Human Rights held in Vienna, Austria, in 1993, had been eagerly awaited around the world by those who wanted new perspectives and understanding to be reflected in the way governments deal with human rights issues. The last such conference had been more than thirty years ago.

The basis of human rights monitoring and activity has changed, especially during the last ten years. The whole United Nations system has grown in response to an increased awareness of human rights, and wider public interest and involvement have brought increased media coverage.

International human rights gatherings in the past were usually compatible discussions between governments and non-governmental communities. The NGOs' international lobbying and advocacy was done by "gray-suited men" approaching similarly gray-suited men on the government side. There were even accusations that the NGOs were in collusion with the governments to suppress the real pain and scandal of human rights violations — or that they had been co-opted into the governments' way of thinking.

All that changed in the 1980s, when the number of NGOs involved in political, social, and economic research and advocacy doubled — even tripled. Maybe the glaring scandal of apartheid helped to educate us. It was not possible to misunderstand that the denial of political and economic rights was also a denial of basic human rights for the South African majority. This glaring case study of the constitutional denial of human rights led to international support for liberation movements.

Such support was a very serious step. In supporting the liberation movements of Southern Africa, the World Council of Churches (WCC) became involved in painful and sometimes bitter debate within its own membership,

THE REV. BOB SCOTT works with the World Council of Churches Programme to Combat Racism, having responsibility for racism and minority issues in Europe, Asia, and the Pacific. Before moving to the WCC in 1988 Bob developed the first Program on Racism for the Conference of Churches in Aotearoa-New Zealand.

Preamble to the
Universal Declaration of Human Rights

WHEREAS recognition of the inherent dignity and of the equal and inalienable rights of all members of the human family is the foundation of freedom, justice and peace in the world,

WHEREAS disregard and contempt for human rights have resulted in barbarous acts which have outraged the conscience of mankind, and the advent of a world in which human beings shall enjoy freedom of speech and belief and freedom from fear and want has been proclaimed as the highest aspiration of the common people,

WHEREAS it is essential, if man is not to be compelled to have recourse, as a last resort, to rebellion against tyranny and oppression, that human rights should be protected by the rule of law,

WHEREAS it is essential to promote the development of friendly relations between nations,

WHEREAS the peoples of the United Nations have in the Charter reaffirmed their faith in fundamental human rights, in the dignity and worth of the human person and in the equal rights of men and women and have determined to promote social progress and better standards of life in larger freedom,

WHEREAS Member States have pledged themselves to achieve, in cooperation with the United Nations, the promotion of universal respect for and observance of human rights and fundamental freedoms,

WHEREAS a common understanding of these rights and freedoms is of the greatest importance for the full realization of this pledge,

NOW, THEREFORE, The General Assembly proclaims this Universal Declaration of Human Rights as a common standard of achievement for all peoples and all nations, to the end that every individual and every organ of society, keeping this Declaration constantly in mind, shall strive by teaching and education to promote respect for these rights and freedoms and by progressive measures, national and international, to secure their universal and effective recognition and observance, both among peoples of Member States themselves and among the peoples of territories under their jurisdiction.

risking even the loss of some of its member churches. But it did not deviate from its position.

The Roman Catholic Church was similarly challenged. Some priests in Latin America abandoned their traditional position of non-involvement in political issues and called for support as they expressed solidarity with, and sometimes even joined, guerrilla freedom fighters. The ensuing debate about liberation theology was an institutional struggle about the consequences of taking up arms to defend oneself in the face of human rights violations. How often did we hear different forms of the question: "What do you do when your family lies dead around you and the perpetrators of the violence are coming back again?"

Too often, it seems, we have defended our own fundamental freedoms of, for example, applauded the heroism of the resistance movement in France during World War II. Yet we have been reluctant to accord Africans or Latin Americans the same right to protect themselves.

Times have indeed changed. Apartheid has been declared a sin, and those churches in South Africa that justified the continuation of apartheid have been labeled heretical. In 1968, when the WCC pledged to combat racism, it was an unusually assertive aspiration for the international ecumenical family. Today, because the television screen brings us instant dramas from South Africa and elsewhere around the globe, many more people understand what it means to have to fight to preserve freedoms so often taken for granted.

Television camera crews cannot film the torture chambers or the interrogation rooms; they cannot be in every village overrun by vicious troops as they pillage, rape, and destroy. Nevertheless, we have a clear picture. What news cameras cannot provide, television dramas do.

With this new public awareness has come increasing public pressure for action by international institutions. Sadly, this has not been matched by an increase in effective action by UN member states to preserve human rights or to bring violators to justice. In 1992, Amnesty International declared: "The United Nations is critically failing to address some of the most fundamental violations of human rights which are still occurring on a horrifying scale in the world today." This is a very strong accusation in light of the complicated network of mechanisms within the United Nations system designed to preserve human rights.

Human Rights Monitoring in the UN

The Commission on Human Rights (CHR) is the UN body directly responsible for monitoring human rights, recommending new international standards, and investigating violations. The fifty-three member states on the commission meet for six weeks at the beginning of each year and report to the Economic and Social Council of the UN (ECOSOC), which is accountable to the UN General Assembly.

The CHR's Sub-Commission on the Discrimination and Protection of Minorities meets for six weeks in the middle of the year. It has a number of working groups. In 1970, ECOSOC adopted Resolution 1503, which provided for receiving reports "regarding consistent and gross violations of human rights and fundamental freedoms by governments." The sub-commission set up the Working Group on Communications, which hears from many thousands of persons and groups whose rights have been violated. The working group meets in secret to consider a number of them, so as to protect those who have provided the evidence.

Other committees that have been created under ECOSOC to address UN conventions and covenants include the Human Rights Committee (HRC), the Committee on the Elimination of All Forms of Racial Discrimination (CERD), the Committee on Economic, Social and Cultural Rights (CESCR), the Committee Against Torture (CAT), the Committee on the Rights of the Child (CRC), and the Committee on the Elimination of Discrimination Against Women (CEDAW). Their main task is receiving reports from governments on their implementation of the conventions and covenants.

The UN also offers assistance and advice to governments that want to improve their ability to protect human rights. "Advisory Services" has been exploited by some governments that continue to abuse human rights while penitently seeking the UN's advice on improving them.

Every year hundreds of UN hours are devoted to the study and discussion of human rights; millions of words are delivered in speeches and a considerable amount of UN funds is spent on the meetings and investigations. How then can Amnesty International say that the UN has failed?

To answer this question requires an understanding of what the United Nations is and how it works. It is a forum of nation states united under a common charter. Signed in San Francisco in 1945, that charter committed the member states to a vast range of collective discussions, procedures, and actions. Respect for human rights was one of the founding principles.

Within the UN, each member state retains its own integrity as a sovereign nation; each has the right to expect that other member states will respect that sovereignty and not intrude on its internal affairs without permission. Consequently, people working on human rights issues on behalf of the UN often find themselves dealing with difficult, time-consuming procedures, delaying tactics, and/or inadequate funds.

Governments may say they want to protect human rights, but they continue to violate them. Governments may say they want abusers of human rights to be brought to account, but they do not mean to include themselves. Governments may declare their commitment to the eradication of human rights violations, but they turn a blind eye to the abuses of member states with whom they have treaty or trade agreements. The commitments look good on paper, but the political reality is sometimes very different.

Human Rights Instruments and Their Present Status

Human Rights Instrument	United States		Canada		Entered
	Signed	Ratified	Signed	Ratified	into force
International Covenant on Economic, Social and Cultural Rights	yes	no	yes	yes	1976
International Covenant on Civil and Political Rights	yes	yes	yes	yes	1976
Optional Protocol to the International Covenant on Civil and Political Rights	no	no	yes	yes	1976
Convention on the Prevention and Punishment of the Crime of Genocide	yes	yes	yes	yes	1951
Convention on the Non-Applicability of Statutory Limitations to War Crimes and Crimes Against Humanity	no	no	no	no	1970
International Convention on the Elimination of All Forms of Racial Discrimination	yes	yes	yes	yes	1970
Convention Relating to the Status of Refugees	yes	yes	yes	yes	1967
Convention Relating to the Status of Stateless Persons	no	no	no	no	1960
Convention on the Reduction of Statelessness	no	no	yes	yes	1975
Convention on the Political Rights of Women	yes	yes	yes	yes	1954
Convention on the Nationality of Married Women	no	no	yes	yes	1958
Convention on the Consent to Marriage, Minimum Age for Marriage, and Registration of Marriages	yes	no	no	no	1964
Convention on the International Right of Correction	no	no	no	no	1962
Slavery Convention of Sept. 25, 1926 as amended	yes	yes	yes	yes	1955
Protocol Amending the Slavery Convention Signed at Geneva on Sept. 25, 1926	yes	yes	yes	yes	1953
Supplementary Convention on the Abolition of Slavery and Slave Trade, Institutions and Practices Similar to Slavery	yes	yes	yes	yes	1957
Convention for the Suppression of the Traffic of Persons and the Exploitation of the Prostitution of Others	no	no	no	no	1951
Convention Against Torture and Other Cruel, Inhuman, or Degrading Punishment	no	no	yes	yes	1951
International Convention on the Suppression and Punishment of the Crime of Apartheid	no	no	no	no	1976
Convention on the Elimination of All Forms of Discrimination Against Women	yes	no	yes	yes	1981
Convention on the Rights of the Child	yes	no	yes	yes	1990

Political will was mustered quickly for a boycott of the Moscow Olympic Games and for the economic boycott against Libya for shielding the alleged perpetrators of the Lockerbie air disaster. But member states' support is denied in seemingly similar situations in other parts of the world.

Why was it relatively easy for the United States to persuade many of the member states to support an intervention in Somalia against the so-called warlord Aidid, and yet not support a similar intervention in Liberia, where the landing of even a small platoon of U.S. soldiers, already waiting off the shore, could have changed that situation dramatically? Why were the pleas for help from beleaguered Tamils in the north and east of Sri Lanka denied while, within days, similar pleas from Kuwaitis were responded to with a massive international force, resulting in the Gulf War?

Of course, every situation is different. But if the United Nations Declaration on Human Rights means anything, surely it cannot matter how many people are involved? As Nelson Mandela said, "If one is hurt we are damaged; if one is not free none of us is free."

So why is the political will of the UN — the energy of member states to do something effective at the right time — so selective? Certainly this is what Amnesty International is saying.

There have been times when, as part of a lobbying team at some UN meeting or other, I have been stunned by the fickleness of international negotiations. Just when we thought we had succeeded in persuading a majority of delegates to act on a specific issue, when the diplomats from the major countries seemed ready to speak out strongly, we heard that a back room deal had been struck and the issue side-lined. Perhaps a crucial number of member states had reconsidered their action in return for future support for one of their own proposals on an entirely unrelated matter. Or perhaps some deceptive argument was swallowed by those who, in the previous hours, seemed convinced to take action.

One example of this problem is the reluctance of the UN in bringing Sri Lanka to account within the Commission on Human Rights. The continuing tragedy of civil war in that country includes violations of human rights by both government and Tamil separatists. No one doubts that. Many NGOs have campaigned for stronger resolutions against the Sri Lankan government, which must be held accountable for its part in those violations. Certainly the Sri Lankan government fears the prospect of condemnatory UN resolutions, and the effect it would have on negotiations for World Bank and other aid support. Sri Lanka has sent its most seasoned diplomats to Geneva. What arguments could they have used to persuade governments to postpone their critical or punitive action for yet another year?

Apparently, Sri Lankan officials pointed to the fact that their government had welcomed UN committees of investigation in the past and is prepared to welcome them in the future. They argued that Sri Lanka is far more cooperative than other Asian governments under scrutiny, such as China (because of Tibet), Indonesia (because of East Timor), and the undemocratic military regime of Burma. Why treat Sri Lanka as critically as these others? So instead of a condemnatory resolution there was merely a "chairman's statement," encouraging the Sri Lankan government to continue its measures to preserve human rights and assuring it of the consistent vigilance of the commission. The violations in Sri Lanka continue, even as the commission discusses the matter.

You might well imagine the deep frustration of the Sri Lanka witnesses who came to Geneva to tell their stories of continuing human rights violations, when the arguments of the Sri Lankan government officials are given preference.

The Evolution of Human Rights

Let's go back a bit, to trace the evolution of human rights. Early declarations, such as the Magna Carta and the United States Declaration of Independence, focused on civil and political rights — but not for all people. Women and peasants were left out of any direct consideration. By the mid-nineteenth century, there had evolved an understanding that basic rights for everybody needed to be defended and preserved. Of course, these rights were largely ignored as the great colonial empires spread across the globe.

The 1930s saw an increased awareness of other basic rights, such as decent living and working conditions and support from the state in times of hardship. These have been called the second generation of human rights — the economic, social, and cultural rights. My own country, Aotearoa-New Zealand, has the reputation of leading the world in this area.

The trauma of World War II led to the major human rights documents that are now our basic references. They reflect the post-war awareness that peace and human rights are linked.

The United Nations Charter (1945) reaffirmed "faith in fundamental human rights, in the dignity and worth of the human person, in the equal rights of men and women and of nations large and small." The Universal Declaration of Human Rights (1948) echoed this: "Recognition of the inherent dignity and of equal and inalienable rights to all members of the human family is the foundation of freedom, justice and peace in the world."

To work for disarmament is to work for peace. This is obvious. But to pursue justice for those denied their rights is also to work for world peace. Thus came the third generation of human rights: peace, disarmament, the protection of the environment and natural resources, and a new economic order that would preserve the economic stability of nations and their citizens.

The main participants in this pursuit were the so-called developed countries of the North. Most of Africa was still under colonial rule and Latin America was often peripheral to any international forums. In 1950 there were only fifty-one nations in the UN.

The painful controversies surrounding the U.S. involvement in Viet Nam in the 1960s helped the human rights debate. Even in Aotearoa-New Zealand, the dialogue on whether or not we should be associated with the U.S. in Viet Nam prompted profound questioning of our national values and priorities.

Out of the turmoil of peace marches and divisions within families a new generation emerged, committed to a more radical understanding of freedom within one's own political or religious beliefs, freedom to live in one's own particular lifestyle without the interference or condemnation of others.

The Soviet invasion of Czechoslovakia also had a profound effect on the evolution of human rights. The global community was horrified by the sight of tanks rolling through the city streets. We shed tears of sadness and helplessness at the loss of freedom for the Czech people. The Sharpeville massacre in South Africa was a similar experience. Who could doubt that the pain of these human rights violations was being felt all over the world?

Since then there has been progress in some areas, the most noticeable being increased recognition of the rights of women. Another is the rights of children — so often the innocent victims of conflicts they are too young to know anything about. There will soon be a Declaration on the Rights of Peoples — a document debated and molded for the last ten years by representatives of peoples from around the world within one of the working groups of the Sub-Commission on Prevention of Discrimination and Protection of Minorities. This declaration could be one of the success stories of the United Nations.

While previous emphasis has been on the preservation of rights of individuals, there has been little reference to collective rights. The traditions of indigenous peoples, however, invariably emphasize group or tribal rights over those of the individual. The close relationship with Mother Earth is the very basis of a spiritual understanding of one's self. The individual is only part of the whole creation.

Racism as a Violation of Human Rights

No discussion of UN priorities would be complete without reference to racism. Racism has been a grave concern for the United Nations for many

---

UN International Decades

1983–1992	United Nations Decade of Disabled Persons
1983–1993	Second Decade to Combat Racism and Racial Discrimination
1985–1996	Transport and Communications Decade for Asia and the Pacific
1988–1997	World Decade for Cultural Development
1990s	Third Disarmament Decade
1990s	International Decade for Natural Disaster Reduction
1990–1999	United Nations Decade of International Law
1990–2000	International Decade for the Eradication of Colonialism
1991–2000	Fourth United Nations Development Decade
1991–2000	United Nations Decade against Drug Abuse
1991–2000	Second Transport and Communications Decade in Africa
1993–2002	Second Industrial Development Decade for Africa
1993–2002	Asian and Pacific Decade of Disabled Persons
1993–2003	Third Decade to Combat Racism and Racial Discrimination
1994–2004	International Decade of the World's Indigenous Peoples

---

years. In 1970 the Convention on the Elimination of All Forms of Racial Discrimination entered into force. Six years later came the Convention on the Suppression and Punishment of the Crime of Apartheid. From 1983 to 1993, the UN observed the "Second Decade to Combat Racism and Racial Discrimination." The sad fact of the 1980s and early 1990s is the rising tide of racism in so many parts of the world. For those of us who live in Europe, it is painful to see and feel the racial animosity growing around us. Racist ideologies have re-emerged in political parties; neo-fascist groups are proud of their violence, as they seek to rid their towns of those they do not like; my Black friends do not feel safe in the streets of most European capitals, especially at night.

The 1993 session of the UN Human Rights Commission adopted a resolution on measures to combat "contemporary forms of racism, racial discrimination, xenophobia and related intolerance" and assigned a special *rapporteur* to report to the Commission annually for three years. The words of the resolution are somber and urgent:

- Conscious that the scourges of racism and racial discrimination are continually assuming new forms, requiring a periodic re-examination of the methods used to combat them,

- Convinced, however, that racism and racial discrimination, in whatever form, are intensified by conflicts over economic resources, in developed as well as in developing countries, and can best be defeated by a combination of economic, legislative and educational measures,

- Reaffirming, that all human rights and fundamental freedoms, economic, social and cultural, as well as civil and political, are indivisible and interrelated, the Commission

Urges all Governments to undertake immediate measures and to develop strong policies effectively to combat racism and eliminate discrimination.

The rapporteur, Maurice Glélé-Ahanhanzo from Benin, listed in his interim report of February 1994 some new forms of racism, including those against minorities and migrant workers. Despite the efforts made in two official UN decades to eliminate racism and racial discrimination, racism had increased.

The rapporteur can report courageous efforts by some governments to overcome and combat racism, but there is a long way to go. At the 1994 session of the UN Commission on Human Rights it was significant that Germany became the first Western power ever to be called to account for racist practices.

The Future

What reforms are needed? For nearly thirty years there has been a debate about the appointment of a UN High Commissioner for Human Rights. But little was done until the discussion was revitalized at the 1993 Vienna Conference. Amnesty International was one of the many NGOs calling for the establishment of the office of a Special Commissioner for Human Rights. The U.S. delegation led the call. But by the time the office was approved within the General Assembly later that year, its powers had been severely limited, and only time will tell if José Ayala Lasso of Ecuador, the first appointee, can be at all effective.

Other improvements are also needed. The UN Commission on Human Rights has a number of rapporteurs assigned to monitor various countries or specific violations such as "Religious Intolerance," "Extrajudicial, Summary or Arbitrary Executions," "Torture and Other Cruel, Inhuman or Degrading Treatment or Punishment," and "Violence Against Women, Its Causes and Consequences." Committees visit countries and issue reports, but they visit only at the invitation of governments, and their documents, which provide raw data, are rarely distributed beyond the confines of the UN.

The new Human Rights Commissioner would do well to improve the "early warning system" about situations where increased violations of human rights are possible. The commissioner needs to be able to act rapidly and to call on the member states for their rapid response. Sometimes months go by before the UN takes action or even begins its investigations.

The concept of Advisory Services needs to be overhauled. Governments that want help in improving their human rights records and facilities are entitled to assistance but should not use Advisory Services to escape critical judgment from other governments. Another major accomplishment would be to achieve universal ratification of all human rights conventions. Many states, even some of those serving on the UN Commission on Human Rights, have not ratified all conventions. Also, the resources and facilities available for documenting, monitoring, and investigating human rights violations need to be increased many times over. There can be no effective action while the UN Center on Human Rights is so woefully understaffed and underfunded.

But here we come back to the fundamental need for all countries to be vigilant about human rights within their own borders and to exercise their influence when other states are at serious fault.

Developing Political Will

Political will varies from country to country. U.S. policy seems particularly sensitive to public opinion. The White House reportedly measures public response not in numbers of letters, but inches. A pile of letters, telefaxes, or telephone messages that reaches eighteen inches indicates a disturbing trend.

In my own country of only 3.2 million people, we used to say it was easy to create the political will for change: fifty letters to the prime minister in one week was enough to cause a stir and raise questions in Parliament.

In some countries, political will seems the caprice or opinion of a small group, or even an individual. In the U.S., the energy for a political course of action may come from within a particular political party or group of people in power. It comes not only from the "voice of the people," but also from a complicated network of partisan agendas or local constituency priorities. Sometimes it is not clear exactly how an opinion or political will emerges from that complex. Often you wonder if the "voice of the people" is being ignored or compromised.

I remember visiting the U.S. State Department with a delegation of church leaders from Aotearoa-New Zealand. We had come to express the offense and violation we felt at U.S. nuclear intrusion in the Pacific. An official informed us, with great condescension, that as church people we should treat the uncertainty of whether a U.S. warship entering one of our harbors was nuclear-armed as "one of the mysteries of life." Our meeting with him went nowhere; the urgent pleading from a small country meant little in the face of the determined political will of the U.S. administration of the day.

How does change come about? Almost certainly it comes with increased awareness — from a combination of respected public leaders, think-tank intellectuals, and plain ordinary citizens prepared to confront their local and federal politicians. It comes through church leaders adopting resolutions passed by national, state, and local church bodies; it comes from editorials in major newspapers. Sometimes it comes when a national leader offers new insights, new perspectives, or new challenges. It does not happen when major financial interests appear to be threatened or when government strategists have convinced their political bosses to stick to some long-term plan whatever the short-term consequences.

What if all U.S. citizens changed their perception of U.S. power from one of strength that needs to be exerted, like that of some kind of international policeman, to a conviction that such wealth, coupled with power, requires the U.S. to be of service to the rest of the world? What a dramatic change that would bring to the whole world.

To change political will requires the strong personal commitment of a recognizable number of people. Churches help create political will on a particular matter when we demonstrate that our commitment to that issue has led us to change ourselves.

Racism Hearings in North America

Let me cite a specific example. In late 1993, and then in October 1994, a number of hearings were held in U.S. cities to define racism as a violation of human rights. In Washington, Chicago, New York, Oakland, Birmingham, and El Paso, eminent church people from around the world campaigned to dramatize the fact that human rights violations that we so easily recognize in Bosnia-Herzegovina, South Africa, or Guatemala are happening every day in North America too. People of color in the U.S., and the Quebecois in Canada suffer the effects of human rights violations just as Tibetans do at the hands of the Chinese or the East Timorese do in Indonesia or the Ogoni people do in Nigeria.

Those U.S. hearings gained a measure of public and media attention, but the impact came only when there was evidence that the message had indeed changed the way the churches act and think. It was not a question of the churches expecting others to change, but the churches having changed themselves. This is what makes the approach to the politician, the political strategist, or government department head so effective.

As churches, we always work from what we understand to be the gospel imperatives — the basis of living and relating to God and to one another laid down in the testimony of Jesus Christ. This is also the basis for the churches' work on human rights violations.

The very first assembly of the World Council of Churches, held in Amsterdam in 1948, issued a clear message (despite the sexist language of the time): "We have to remind ourselves and all men that God has put down the mighty from their seats and exalted the humble and meek. We have to learn afresh together to speak boldly in Christ's name both to those in power and to the people; to oppose terror, cruelty and race discrimination, to stand by the outcast, the prisoner and the refugee."

There is a challenge there. William Temple, archbishop of Canterbury, wrote years ago that the world will fail to be impressed with the power of the gospel we preach until it sees the power of that gospel to unite the church. I could add, "to unite the church in living out the gospel and struggling together to change those things that are a violation of that gospel."

The gospel directives for our work on human rights are scattered throughout the New Testament. But read particularly the fifteenth chapter of John, where Jesus describes himself as the vine and us as the branches. There is absolutely no doubt that we are called to be with Christ in love and therefore to carry out his commandment of love. And there is no escape. Jesus said, "You did not choose me, but I chose you."

And we are commanded to go all the way. "If the world hates you, be aware that it hated me before it hated you. If you belonged to the world, the world would love you as its own. Because you do not belong to the world, but I have chosen you out of the world, therefore the world hates you." It is hard to hide from the significance of those words.

The church has considerable experience in monitoring and praying to end human rights violations. At the local level, there is hardly a congregation that does not pray weekly for those who are hungry, in distress, homeless, or lonely. In times of crisis, what we read in newspapers is soon translated into our prayers.

Human rights desks in national church offices receive a steady appeal for help from around the world. I remember being told by someone lobbying for economic sanctions against Indonesia after the massacre of more than fifty East Timorese in Dili on November 12, 1991: "I came to you churches first because everything you are about, everything you say, points to the assumption you will understand what I have to say. The politicians, and the others I have to talk to, will be more difficult. But I know the churches will understand."

The truth is that we often are not prepared, not understanding, and not sensitive, preferring to pray about human rights violations rather than to join those seeking to overcome them. This is not to devalue the power of prayer but to recommend the action dimension to which God calls us whenever we pray.

Something we must confront, however, is a little excuse that lingers in the vocabulary of the church and is used whenever we feel fainthearted. We say, "The church must not take sides. We must be the same to everyone. We must be the reconcilers."

Of course, the church has a very responsible ministry of reconciliation. But that means a lot more than sitting in the middle and smiling left and right. In Aotearoa-New Zealand for many years, the response to the scourge of apartheid in South Africa was that we should be "bridge-builders." Even church leaders espoused this. The theory was that by keeping open contact with White South Africa (especially playing our beloved soccer), we would help them understand the importance of changing apartheid. In reality, of course, our "bridge-building" did no such thing. It merely comforted the Whites. Not until we chopped down the bridge — by imposing economic sanctions — did the change we hoped for begin to happen. This reminds me of the Filipino who said that you cannot build a bridge from the middle of the river. You have to choose a side.

Begin Where You Are

So, you ask: How can I possibly know all there is to know so I can be effective? How can I possibly monitor everything? It is a busy life being a Christian if one is expected to cope with all that in addition to what is happening in my own community!"

There is the clue! It is in our homes and local communities that we begin. When, as a church, we are conscious of human rights, individually and collectively, in the local community of which we are a part — we are in training for what is happening far away. And when those links are made, the next step is to commission each other, as Christians, to become more specific. Here are some well-tested action suggestions:

• **Monitoring.** Our own eyes and ears provide us with the data for the local area. Newspapers, radio, and television networks provide national and international highlights, and there is an increasing range of alternative information publications to provide the details. The national staff in our denominations, as well as in the National Council of the Churches of Christ in the USA and in the Canadian Council of Churches and its coalitions, can be called on to help with this. *With All God's People*, the Ecumenical Prayer Cycle of the World Council of Churches, offers brief descriptions of international situations and special needs.

• **Study and reflection.** This requires regular gathering to share the information and explore its implications with prayer and sensitivity. Sometimes we in the church prefer to remain in this phase rather than to take the next step, which is advocacy.

• **Advocacy.** If we understand the details of particular human rights violations, then as Christians we must be advocates for changing those situations. To be silent is to ignore Christ's warning to us: "I was hungry and you gave me no food, I was thirsty and you gave me nothing to drink, I was a stranger and you did not welcome me, naked and you did not clothe me, sick and in prison and you did not visit me....Just as you did not do it to one of the least of these, you did not do it to me" (Matt. 25).

We become advocates by raising awareness of these issues within our own communities and then expressing our views to those who are deciding policy or directing action at the government level.

What has this got to do with the United Nations? Everything! Government delegates speak or vote in the United Nations according to the political will formed in their own countries. Their positions can change with reversals or new perceptions of the political will on that particular matter back home.

The task of working to eradicate human rights violations may be a never-ending one for the United Nations. The cynics might ask, "Why bother?" The victims ask, "Why not?" The followers of Christ have to reply: "We must!"

The General Assembly considering that discrimination against women is incompatible with human dignity and with the welfare of the family and of society...bearing in mind, the great contribution made by women to social, political, economic and cultural life...solemnly proclaims this Declaration:

ARTICLE 1: Discrimination against women, denying or limiting as it does their equality of rights with men, is fundamentally unjust and constitutes an offence against human dignity.
> —*from the Declaration on the Elimination of Discrimination against Women*

•

For in Christ Jesus you are all children of God through faith. As many of you as were baptized into Christ have clothed yourselves with Christ. There is no longer Jew or Greek, there is no longer slave or free, there is no longer male and female; for all of you are one in Christ Jesus. And if you belong to Christ, then you are Abraham's offspring, heirs according to the promise.
> —*Galatians 3:26–29*

– 7 –

Social Reconstruction:
Toward New Roles for Women

Luisa A. S. Vicioso

One very important discovery I have made is the difference between the condition of women and the situation of women. UNICEF, like the churches, has since the 1950s been working on the *conditions* that affect women, such as health, education, and labor. Our work process has looked upon women as objects of our programming, so that in effect we have been doing things for women. We are now trying to move from working for women to working with women, to change their *situations*.

We are now talking about women as the subjects of our programs; they are considered to be the protagonists and/or the heads of our projects — that is, in charge of the projects that affect them. We are talking about the empowerment of women.

Country development programs and theories have always considered women as part of the general society. Our governments had programs and policies for citizens, not for women as a special or a separate part of society. Therefore, development progress for women could not be evaluated, because women were not specified or quantified as a group.

Back in the 1950s, when there was a broad emphasis on development for all (especially in the poorer, underdeveloped regions and countries), it was hoped that the benefits of development programs and industrial investments would trickle down to the poor — and to women. These policies expanded and in the 1960s there was a great emphasis on production and industrialization in Latin America.

After the investment period — which necessarily included loans and

LUISA VICIOSO is UNICEF's National Officer for Women and Educational Programs in the Dominican Republic, director of the Department of Education and Training for the Dominican Family Planning Association, and a consultant to Family Planning International Association. This chapter is adapted from her presentation at a special seminar in 1993 in honor of the thirtieth anniversary of the Church Center for the United Nations in New York City. From 1973 to 1979, Luisa was a seminar designer for the United Methodist Office for the UN.

The United Nations System and the Commission on the Status of Women: Fifty Years of Work for Women

1945   Article 8 of the Charter of the United Nations states: "The United Nations shall place no restrictions on the eligibility of men and women to participate in any capacity and under conditions of equality in its principal and subsidiary organs."

1946   The Sub-Commission on the Status of Women meets for the first time. ECOSOC establishes the full Commission on the Status of Women.

1947   The Commission on the Status of Women holds its first session and establishes relations with the International Labour Organization (ILO), the United Nations Educational, Scientific and Cultural Organization (UNESCO), and nongovernmental organizations.

1951   ILO adopts the Equal Remuneration Convention (No. 100).

1952   The Convention on the Political Rights of Women is adopted.

1957   The Convention on the Nationality of Married Women is adopted.

1960   UNESCO adopts the Convention against Discrimination in Education, followed in 1962 by a protocol setting up a commission to deal with any disputes that might arise between member states party to the convention.

1965   ILO adopts the Employment (Women with Family Responsibilities) Recommendation (No. 123).

1967   The Declaration on the Elimination of Discrimination against Women is adopted.

1968   A Special Rapporteur is appointed to prepare a study on the status of women and family planning.

1974   The Declaration on the Protection of Women and Children in Emergency and Armed Conflict is adopted.

1975   The World Conference of the International Women's Year is held in Mexico City from June 19 to July 2, with the theme, "Equality, Development and Peace," and a World Plan of Action is adopted.

long-term international credit — we in Latin America (one of the affected regions), suddenly discovered in the 1970s that we had gigantic foreign debts. Our countries were subjected to what was called "adjusted progress" by the international lending agencies, and our governments responded to the "economic adjustment" by cutting all social programs. The net effect of this policy was that the poorest of the poor had to make the first payments on the debts that had been incurred by our governments. And who paid the highest price for this "adjustment" in Latin America? Women!

1976–1985   UN Decade for Women: Equality, Development and Peace

1976   The Voluntary Fund for the UN Decade for Women is established. The International Research and Training Institute for the Advancement of Women (INSTRAW) is established.

1977   A special rapporteur is appointed to prepare a study on the influence of the mass communication media on attitudes toward the roles of women and men.

1979   The Convention on the Elimination of All Forms of Discrimination against Women is adopted. The Commission requests the Food and Agriculture Organization of the UN (FAO) and the World Health Organization (WHO) to report to it on a regular basis.

1980   At the mid-point of the Decade, the World Conference of the UN Decade for Women: Equality, Development and Peace with the sub-theme of employment, health, and education, is held in Copenhagen.

1981   ILO adopts the Convention concerning Equal Opportunities and Equal Treatment for Men and Women Workers: Women with Family Responsibilities (No. 156).

1982   The Declaration on the Participation of Women in Promoting International Peace and Cooperation is adopted. A special rapporteur is appointed to prepare a report on the suppression of the traffic in persons and the exploitation of the prostitution of others.

1985   The World Conference to Review and Appraise the Achievements of the UN Decade for Women is held in Nairobi. Nairobi Forward Looking Strategies for the Advancement of Women are adopted. The Voluntary Fund for the Decade becomes the UN Development Fund for Women (UNIFEM).

1990   Recommendations on the advancement of women, violence against women, and concepts of gender equity are forwarded to various world conferences: Environment and Development (Brazil, 1992); Human Rights (Vienna, 1993); and Population and Development (Cairo, 1994). The Commission's work focused on the failure of governments and society to implement the Forward Looking Strategies for the Advancement of Women, rather than on specific acts of discrimination.

1993   Declaration on Violence Against Women is adopted by the General Assembly.

1995   The Fourth World Conference on Women is held in Beijing, China.

The burden fell upon women because of their traditional role in Latin society. Women care for the health of the family; women are in charge of the well-being of the family; women eat less if the cost of food rises. During this period, women had to go out and earn the additional money needed to support the family. During the 1980s alone, 20 million women joined the labor force! By the year 2000, it is estimated there will be 55 million women working. Women are always working, of course, but I refer here to women joining the labor force for money, and thereby increasing the tax base.

UNICEF Model: Latin America

UNICEF, which has always centered its work on children, also recognizes that behind every child is a mother. Until 1976, most of its programs for women were geared to their roles as caretakers of children — encouraging breast-feeding, vaccinations, participating in nutritional programs, and so forth. But UNICEF forgot about the women themselves, as persons.

In 1976, responding to pressure from women, UNICEF created its regional women's program. It began, like many church programs, with a number of small income-generating projects for women, with studies and evaluation, promoting "appropriate technologies." By 1982, there were approximately seventeen projects in Latin America and the Caribbean. At that point, an evaluation revealed that the women's programs were isolated from the rest of UNICEF's program operations. They were very sporadic, dispersed, short-term projects; once UNICEF withdrew, the projects ended. Because of this evaluation, UNICEF's managers changed their strategy. They decided that they didn't know enough about women and had to do more research; but they also resolved to concentrate on basic service programs for women and to continue with health training.

Subsequently, another evaluation resulted in UNICEF's Programs for Women, emphasizing social services and tailored to three major regions. We had learned that the problems in Latin America and the Caribbean are not the same problems that women have in Africa or in Asia. UNICEF leaders have come to understand that when they decide to change a global goal, they have to think of how that change will be adapted to the different regions.

I myself am part of a team that designs strategies for the women's programs in Latin America and the Caribbean. We evaluate and make changes as necessary. I'll give you an example.

A program was started in Peru called "Social Mobilization Program for Women." For poor women at the grassroots level, it used children's health issues to motivate women's involvement. It was a massive program; thousands of women joined, and it was presented as a model program for the entire region. I went to evaluate it, asked the women some questions, and got responses like these:

Q: Who's doing the housework now?

A: The eldest daughter.

Q: How are men participating in the program?

A: They don't.

Q: How do you manage with your husband?

A: Well, he's very good; he doesn't beat me when I get home now.

The answers made me realize that in terms of the life of women, this program was not making a difference. Involving women in a program doesn't necessarily mean that their lives are improved; sometimes life is more burdensome, because the traditional tasks must still be accomplished. To whom did they pass these tasks? To the eldest daughter.

In effect, therefore, this program was indirectly contributing to that child's exploitation. So we advised the program leaders that the idea would work only if they encouraged women to re-examine their positions. We have to encourage shared domestic work, because it is not practical for women to join the labor force and still have to cook, clean, and serve their families at home. What does the man do at home? We have to promote equality in domestic work. We also have to promote equality in child-raising. Why don't we encourage men to take their children to be vaccinated? Why don't we ask these questions in the Evaluation Manual? Why don't we put these questions in the Training Manual? Why do we perpetuate women's traditional roles? Unless we ask these questions, the attitudes will not change, and we will contribute only to making the women's lives more difficult.

What, specifically, are we struggling for in the Latin American and Caribbean region? I will present some examples, based on our priorities in the Dominican Republic.

Women's Ideas of Their Role in Society

We are trying to change women's "gender perspectives" — their own view of being a woman — so they will understand that the role they play in society is socially constructed. If women do not come to understand that their role is built through the value system of the schools, the churches, the community, and society, they will not be able to change their situations.

If women think that their roles are God-given or are bound by cultural tradition ("We are born to get married and born to have children; and our place is in the home"), then there is no room for change. On the other hand, if women understand that roles are socially constructed, then they can work for equity with men and can struggle to change their roles.

Here is an example of social construction as it exists in the Dominican Republic. Women are 50 percent of the population and 52 percent of the electorate. But when we look at our society and the power structure, we see this: In Congress, out of 150 senators and deputies, we have only 14 women. In government positions of power we have only 2 women, the Minister of Education and the Minister of Health — out of a total of 45 positions! In the Ministry of Education, 85 percent of the teachers are women, yet the higher the level, the fewer the women. The Inspector, the Regional Director — the people in charge — are all men. When we look at our whole society in that way, we realize women have very little power in the Dominican Republic. So the first thing for women to do is to understand that they are a force that can work to change the power structure.

One important area we must examine and correct is the position of women within the laws. In the Dominican Republic, we are still ruled by what is called the Napoleonic Code, which dates from 1804. Under the Civil Code (the code that rules relationships concerning property), men in the Dominican Republic can give away, mortgage, or sell properties without notifying their wives. Under the Penal Code we have an article called "Excusability of Homicide by Adultery." In the Dominican Republic, only women are "adulterers," because for men adultery is considered culturally acceptable. So only women are "justifiably killed" when adultery is suspected. The law excuses men, so they can kill their wives but avoid prison if adultery is involved. We are trying to change this legislation.

Further, under the Penal Code, the penalty for rape varies according to the age of the victim. If you rape a one-year-old child, you are given twenty years; if you rape a six-year-old child, you are given fifteen years; a thirteen-year-old, maybe five years; and if you rape *me*, it is not a crime — because I, a grown woman, somehow provoked it. We are trying to change this type of legislation, which affects women so negatively.

We are pushing for a "National Policy" that identifies women as a specific group. Then when the government proposes a development plan for all Dominicans, we will be able to ask, "How will women participate in agriculture, in labor, in health, and in education?" And when we want to evaluate the progress of the Dominican government in terms of its inclusiveness of women, we will have the indicators to do so.

We are working on "gender education" with the Ministry of Education through an institution called the Department of Women's Education. We plan to train twenty-four thousand teachers in gender awareness and are reviewing curricula for all educational levels (pre-school, primary school, high school, and college). We are also reviewing the textbooks for sexual stereotyping and sexist language. This is a very important issue because every teacher influences several generations.

Changing the Social Construction

Women perform roles that society doesn't acknowledge. We are now making efforts to calculate the economic value of socializing and raising children. If women recognize the value of their roles, they then have a bargaining tool for claiming a power position in society and being full participants in determining the direction in which society should move.

We began the work of UNICEF's Women's Program in the Dominican Republic in 1986 by supporting the Women's Bureau (a government-supported entity) with our vision of women as a political force. We held a seminar in which women from different political affiliations learned that regardless of politics, we had common problems as women. Subsequently, we held a seminar on the participation of women in the electoral process, and out of that came a common platform of twelve points for political parties and the government. But this didn't happen without resistance. Three directors of the Women's Bureau were fired in the process.

Of course, we have had women in power, but not all women are equal, and we have had some very bad examples of women in power. They have learned the rules of the game as practiced by men. So we must work with women to promote a different set of values.

Another phenomenon in the context of politics is the "failure of the left" in Latin America during the 1980s. Women joined community organizations in large numbers in an attempt to solve day-to-day problems created by the failure of socialist or communist governments. These large groups are a political force, but the question remains of how to move women from dealing with basic food and housing problems to thinking of themselves as a power base.

I have been asked if there are class or cultural differences in teaching gender awareness. Upper-class, middle-class, and lower-class women are all subjected to the same kind of socialization. Upper-class women have advantages; they have maids who take care of children, cook, and clean the house. But that represents no change in the roles women perform in society. One woman is simply passing the task on to another woman. Gender stereotyping cuts across classes, in that sense.

There is resistance, however, when we go into communities and tell poor women, "Look, you are oppressed, and your husband is part of the problem," because we leave and they stay. Before they came to the workshops, they were leading their lives and coping with their husbands. We give them a new perspective; but they have to go back to the same old situation, now aware of their oppression. And so they ask, "Now what?" If they want to struggle against the situation, they have no alternatives. The men will leave them and will not support the children.

Another cultural issue is that of ethnic or racial difference. I remember when the feminist movement began, we Latin women were very much against it, because the movement started as a middle-class White women's phenomenon. Those women came to tell us, Latin and Black women, that we were oppressed. We knew it. And then they came to tell us that our men were oppressing us. We knew that too. Our problem was that we understood racism — and we couldn't side with our racist oppressors against our sexist oppressors. Of course we now know that middle-class White men are as macho as Black and Latin men; but back then, Black and Latin women felt that if they were to join the feminist movement they would be contributing to the negative stereotypes of Black and Latin men.

So we said no. We will handle our problem with our men. Our grandmothers taught us to have our arguments or conflicts with our men "between the bedroom door and the bed." Never take domestic issues out in public, because they become more complicated. So we couldn't join the mainstream because we were dealing with a larger problem — racism — and we had to deal with that first. Whenever we attempt to help other women raise their consciousness, we have to remember it is their society and try to work with them in that context.

Religion: Issues Affecting Women

The church and state in Latin America are predominantly Roman Catholic, and the church is in opposition to several important issues we are working on to support and protect women. In the campaign for legal modifications, we introduced a bill under the Health Code, which would change the law to permit therapeutic abortions. If you were the mother of three children and knew another pregnancy would endanger your life, you would be able to get an abortion because your priority is the other three children. But the Catholic Church is against this. For women in Latin America this means, in effect, that their lives are less valuable than the life of the unborn.

I do not approve of abortion as a means of birth control. Middle-class women, with access to family planning, do not usually have to subject their bodies to this violence. But poor women in rural areas, in the swamps of Santo Domingo, are dying like flies because they don't have access to family planning; and the church is against family planning. The poor women in these areas don't have access to a "proper Catholic upbringing," which teaches the "rhythm method," and the church doesn't even provide them with charts to define it. So who's dying? The poorest of the poor. Abortion is one of the leading causes of death among adolescent females in Latin America and the Caribbean. Still the church maintains its position against family planning and advocates the elimination of all sex education. This relates to the issue of AIDS, because the church is against the use of condoms.

Because of our campaigns on the legal issues, the pope's representative and the cardinal wrote to UNICEF, cautioning it not to "get involved" in these issues. But in the capital of Santo Domingo alone, we have forty-five thousand street children. So our response was, "Fine, we understand and agree with your concerns for the children that haven't been born, but we are more worried about the forty-five thousand in the streets!" And we ask ourselves, "Why doesn't the church play a more active role in creating employment and education centers for those children? They have the money to do it."

UNICEF: A Changing Vision

Because UNICEF centers its programming philosophy on the child, the main emphases of health programs for women are maternity, with prenatal and postnatal care, and breastfeeding. Tuberculosis is the main cause of death among young women in the Dominican Republic, though, and gynecological cancer is third, so we have to deal with them too. Likewise with mental health problems.

Because of the economic crisis in the Dominican Republic, masses of women have had to join the labor force to supplement the family income. In addition, they must provide all the social services the government no longer provides (health care, education, nutrition). The price for this double burden is the deterioration of mental health. Last year, 90 percent of eight thousand calls to the Institute for the Prevention of Suicide were from women. We also have experienced a great increase in violence against women — the sixth highest cause of death for women in the Dominican Republic.

So now we have included the problems of violence and stress in our National Campaign on Women's Health. This is an innovation for UNICEF. The new directions — policy-making, modifying laws that affect women, gender awareness training, and women's health issues — represent the core of the program that we're advocating in the Dominican Republic and in the rest of Latin America and the Caribbean.

This progress hasn't taken place without resistance. To help UNICEF change, we are retraining all its staff in gender perspective, teaching health officers that women have to be an integral part of program planning, and training communications officers to make women's causes their cause.

We are bringing this message to Latin American women: "Look, we have the greatest advantage. We, as mothers, teach our cultural values to the very society with which we are struggling; that gives us the power to influence change in that society." This is the beginning of "social reconstruction," the wave of the future.

WHEREAS the child, by reason of his physical and mental immaturity, needs special safeguards and care including appropriate legal protection, before as well as after birth...

WHEREAS mankind owes the child the best it has to give,

Now, THEREFORE, the General Assembly proclaims this Declaration of the Rights of the Child to the end that he may have a happy childhood and enjoy for his own good and for the good of society the rights and freedoms herein set.... The child, for the full and harmonious development of his personality, needs love and understanding.

—*from the United Nations Declaration of the Rights of the Child*

•

Then little children were being brought to him in order that he might lay his hands on them and pray. The disciples spoke sternly to those who brought them; but Jesus said, "Let the little children come to me, and do not stop them; for it is to such as these that the kingdom of heaven belongs." And he laid his hands on them and went on his way.

—*Matthew 19:13–15*

8

Promises to the Children of the World: Africa's Children

Lindiwe Chaza-Jangira

It is necessary to revisit events of the past, in order to more fully understand present situations and to determine the appropriate course of action for the future. Africa today encompasses fifty-three sovereign states. They are polit-ically independent, but for most, economic independence is still an illusion. This is due, in part, to the multinational and foreign control of resources; uneven terms of trade; the debt crisis; lack of training; and to some extent absence of the political will among the powerful to change the situation. Af-rica is in a state of unrest due to internal political differences and economic pressures that are a direct result of colonialism. During the post-World War I period, colonial powers, in their quest to expand their empires, fought over African territory, and the victors indiscriminately carved up the continent for themselves.

They gave no consideration to the natural divisions or rules of coexistence already established in Africa. Foreign languages, standards, and values were imposed on the indigenous peoples without regard for their various traditions, histories, and cultures. Traditional coping mechanisms of the people eroded as they struggled to conform to the demands of their colonizers. Borders were drawn, splitting families and rearranging tribal and ethnic boundaries. Whole villages were displaced, as their lands were used for mining and farming by the new settlers. Many of the territorial disputes taking place in Africa to-day have to do with retracing and reclaiming the traditional boundaries of precolonial times.

The relationship between Europe and the African colonies was based on trade. The colonies gave Europe access to raw materials and a market for

Since 1987, LINDIWE CHAZA-JANGIRA of Zimbabwe has worked with UNIFEM (UN Fund for Women), UNDP (UN Development Program), and UNICEF (UN Children's Fund). She has been responsible for program development in areas such as maternal and child health; child survival, protection, and development; and emergency management for women and children in especially difficult circumstances.

its manufactured products. Colonists used the industrial advances of the nineteenth century to develop ports and transportation systems in order to facilitate movement of goods and enslaved people from Africa. There was no investment in infrastructure to directly benefit the indigenous peoples. One exception was the railroad system, the only major transportation system built on the continent. This was intended to run from "Cape to Cairo" (from the Cape of Good Hope in South Africa to Egypt) to facilitate travel by settlers and commercial movement of Africa's abundant natural resources such as gold, ivory, and cocoa.

The arrival of the missionaries marked the first attempt to provide any kind of services to benefit the local people. Churches, schools, and hospitals were established. Out of necessity, some basic infrastructure was built.

As African nations began to develop, Western patterns, such as the accumulation of wealth by a very few and systems of government that did little to meet the needs of the population at large, became the norm. Preferential treatment of minority groups within societies widened divisions between various tribes and ethnic groups. This situation was intensified by financial support from Western nations that had no vested interest in developing Africa for Africa's sake but profited from the continental destabilization and continuing conflicts.

Children as Victims

During the decade 1980–1990, the children of Africa had a particularly difficult experience. Angola, Mozambique, and other countries were in a state of war, while Namibia and Zimbabwe were just recovering from many years of fighting wars for independence.

These wars were fought both in towns and rural areas, destroying what little infrastructure and services were in place. Many productive activities were interrupted, and villagers were often forced to flee their homes, leaving all belongings. The majority (approximately 200 million) have limited resources and are extremely poor. The poorest of the poor are women, who often head households while their husbands go to the cities in search of work. Children, therefore, often grow up without both parents and are deprived of basic health and education services because the household income is not sufficient to support these.

Millions of children across Africa find themselves in circumstances that would be considered too harsh for an adult to withstand, let alone a child. Still, they struggle to survive, doing whatever may be necessary (and often deemed "unholy") to survive from one uncertain day to the next. The root of their difficulties is poverty, although the immediate causes of their predicaments vary.

Women and children are always the innocent victims of war, displaced from their homes as armies pass through, looking for food and shelter. The emotional strain of that displacement reduces the ability of mothers to care for their children, especially with no source of food or income.

There are reportedly more than 20 million refugees and displaced persons in Africa today, and the number continues to rise with each new conflict. There have been massive movements of women and children to neighboring countries, escaping political and/or religious persecution or fleeing from the terror of war.

The inevitable and accelerated progression of the Sahara Desert from the north, changes in climatic conditions, and the impact of environmental destruction in general have resulted in a series of droughts affecting the northern, eastern, and southern sectors of the continent. In the mid-1980s, these droughts caused a serious famine that killed more than a million people, mostly women and children dependent on the land for their livelihood. The urban poor were also affected, since they could not afford the high prices of food.

In 1991 and 1992, a severe drought also hit Southern Africa, affecting an estimated 18 million people. Childhood diseases associated with drought, such as malnutrition, measles, diarrhea, and other water-related diseases, increased. Through the quick response of the Southern African governments, under the auspices of the Southern Africa Development Community (SADC), as well as the cooperation of donors and United Nations agencies, a major catastrophe was averted. Food, water, and medicines were targeted to the most vulnerable — women and children — and distributed throughout the region. Special feeding was provided for children in schools, and for infants and younger children at clinics and health posts.

Child Soldiers

The various territorial and ethnic disputes in many countries on the African continent have turned thousands of children into killing machines. Some children are lured by the availability of food, clothing, and shelter. The army provides a home that, ironically, gives them a sense of security.

Young children who have witnessed their family members being killed or who have been forced to actually commit the atrocities themselves often feel a sense of solidarity with the military forces of the opposite camp, and the army becomes their family and their home. There are those who join the military for adventure, but a large number are kidnapped (from their homes

UN International Conferences

1990   World Summit for Children

1992   UN Conference on Environment and Development

1993   World Conference on Human Rights

1994   International Conference on Population and Development

Global Conference on the Sustainable Development of Small Island Developing States

World Conference on Natural Disaster Reduction

1995   Fourth World Conference on Women: Action for Equality, Development and Peace

World Summit for Social Development

Conference of the Parties to the UN Framework Convention on Climate Change

Review Conference on the Treaty on the Non-Proliferation of Nuclear Weapons

Ninth UN Congress on the Prevention of Crime and the Treatment of Offenders

1996   UN Conference on Human Settlements (Habitat II)

or schools, while at play, or while tending the herds) and forced to join the army against their will.

The recruitment of children under the age of fifteen to engage in military combat is not a new phenomenon. During the course of my work with UNICEF, I met with such children. The most vivid of those experiences were in Liberia and Sierra Leone. In one interview, a boy soldier admitted being very proud of the role he was playing in shaping his country. He felt no remorse for the people he had killed — including old people, women, and little babies. He did his job with pride and felt he was favored because of his swiftness and accuracy in "taking out the enemy." He told me that he would like to go back to school, but was not ready to do this right away — because he wanted one more chance to experience the excitement of the war front.

In a home for war-affected children in Liberia, supported by UNICEF and some local NGOs, I met seventy-five boys no more than thirteen years of age who were ex-combatants. It was shocking to see the kind of psychological scars the war had left on most of them. They were receiving trauma counseling, being sensitized to peace education and conflict resolution, and learning vocational skills that would prepare them for re-entry and survival in society.

Street Children and Working Children

Traditional attitudes with regard to bearing children in order to have a readily available labor force are still prevalent throughout Africa. In contrast to Europe, which moved from child labor in the coal mines to children in classrooms, in post-World War II Africa children continue to work — though many have moved from the fields to the streets. Of the estimated 10 million street children in Africa, most are boys.

Poverty and increased urbanization are major determinants of whether children go to school or try to survive by begging, stealing, or working. It is not enough for education to be free and compulsory if serious measures are not taken to alleviate poverty. It is hard for suffering people to foresee that they will be better off in the long run if their children go to school rather than work to put food on the table today.

Working children spend all day in the streets or shops or markets; but at the end of the day they have a home to return to, however humble. Street children, on the other hand, constantly roam the city, begging, stealing, or doing odd jobs; at the end of the day they find a place on the sidewalk to go to sleep. They have no real families except the other children on the street. Some have been abandoned because their families can no longer afford to care for them; others sought to escape physical and sexual abuse in the home. In the streets many are sexually exploited, as both boys and girls are forced into prostitution.

Years of investment in infrastructure have not been matched by development of the vocational capacity to run the systems necessary to cope with this situation. There is, therefore, a major campaign to develop human resources through vocational training and adult literacy classes.

Health and Sanitation

The number of children who die each year in Africa has been estimated at almost 5 million. The majority are under the age of five. African children continue to die from diseases that have not posed serious threats to children in Europe or North America since 1900 — measles, whooping cough, malaria, malnutrition, and polio. These are all "preventable" diseases, yet attempts to wipe them out in Africa have proved futile. Providing a "cure" without transferring medical knowledge and building the capacity to immunize ignores the root of the problem.

As Africa continues to battle diseases that are preventable, the continent's rates of population growth and infant and child mortality remain higher than those of Asia and Latin America. The global AIDS epidemic threatens to multiply the number of African children dying. Many are already AIDS orphans. Having lost their parents to the disease, their own chances of survival are very slim, even if they do not contract the illness. For the same reasons that common preventable diseases have not been conquered in Africa, the incidence of AIDS and AIDS-related deaths in Africa will quickly outnumber that on other continents.

International Accords

The end of the 1980s ushered in a new decade and new hopes for Africa's children, beginning with the adoption of the Convention on the Rights of the Child. Following that, the declaration of a World Summit for Children and the Dakar Consensus gave strong indications that governments were seriously concerned about the future of Africa's children. The Convention on the Rights of the Child, initiated by UNICEF and the United Nations Center for Human Rights and adopted by the United Nations General Assembly on November 20, 1989, contains fifty-four articles. Articles 1 through 41 deal with the survival, development, and protection of children. Important excerpts follow:

- A child is recognized as a person under eighteen years of age unless national law recognizes the age of majority earlier.
- Every child has the inherent right to life, and the state has an obligation to ensure the child's survival and development.
- The state shall protect the child from all forms of maltreatment, by parents or others responsible for the care of the child; and establish appropriate social programs for the prevention of abuse and the treatment of victims.
- The child has a right to the highest standards of health and medical care possible. The state must ensure that primary health care, preventive health care, public health education, and the reduction of infant mortality are given priority.
- The child has a right to education, and it is the state's responsibility to ensure that primary education is free and compulsory, to encourage different forms of secondary education accessible to every child, and to make higher education available.
- Education shall aim to develop the child's personality, talents, and mental and physical capabilities to the fullest extent. It should prepare a child for an active adult life, fostering respect for his, her, and others' cultural identity, language, cultural background and values.
- The child has a right to be protected from work that threatens his/her health, education, or development. The state must set minimum ages for employment and regulate working conditions.

- The state has the responsibility to protect the child from drug abuse, sexual exploitation, sale, trafficking, and abduction.
- States shall take all feasible measures to ensure that children under fifteen years of age have no direct part in hostilities. No child below fifteen shall be recruited into the armed forces. States shall also ensure the protection and care of children who are affected by armed conflict.

What must be advocated now is the adoption and implementation of national policies to support these rights. The establishment of child survival, protection, and development programs has been a sign of good intent on the part of many African governments, and universal ratification of the Convention on the Rights of the Child is expected. However, financial and human resource constraints may limit efforts to monitor and enforce adherence to the convention.

For two days in September 1990, almost a year after the adoption of the Convention on the Rights of the Child, the World Summit for Children was convened in New York. It had been recorded as the largest gathering of world leaders in history, until the 1995 World Summit for Social Development, which drew 188 heads of state. At this summit, of the 71 countries represented by a head of state or a ministerial level official, 16 were African. Another 28 African nations were represented by a state observer. All publicly declared their commitment to allocating national resources for the survival, protection, and development of children.

Under the auspices of the Organization for African Unity (OAU), the International Conference on Assistance to African Children was convened in Dakar, Senegal, in November 1992. The Dakar Consensus was a giant leap forward as African governments reaffirmed their commitment to necessary changes in policy on behalf of Africa's children. They went a step further and recognized the vital role that women play in African society, stating that unless a serious and concerted effort is made to address issues such as the status of women, war and peace, and the need for social services such as health and education, Africans would not begin to improve the current state of Africa's children.

The Girl Child

Being born a girl in Africa decreases the already marginal chances of surviving to one's fifth birthday. Traditionally, a baby boy has been more welcome than a girl, because boys continue the family bloodline. Girls are not of much value, except to help with household chores and eventually to bear sons. Since limited family resources usually are invested in boys, the chances of girls going to school have until now been almost nonexistent. Girls are married off as soon as they reach puberty and are expected to continue bearing children until menopause.

African females are pregnant most of their lives, but most are unable to provide their children with adequate nutrition or meet their other basic needs. The frequency of pregnancies also results in many miscarriages, complications in childbirth, and often the death of the young mothers. Taboos associated with sex and reproduction often leave young girls with no one to turn to discuss their sexuality. Girls often find themselves being sexually abused both inside and outside of the home, frequently by family members, but must suffer silently.

Since the World Summit for Children and the Dakar Consensus, African governments now are making special provisions for the girl child.

The Role of the Church

Religion has always had a major role to play in African society. Today, most societies practice the Christian faith or follow the teachings of Muhammad. Alongside these beliefs, they look to the ancestors for guidance and redemption from the ravages of war, poverty, and famine. Africans always have turned to a higher spiritual entity for consolation and for alternatives to earthly solutions.

Churches in Africa can help communicate information vital to the survival and protection of African children. Church buildings are used not only for worship, but as forums for discussing all issues concerning the community. Attempts should be made to initiate development programs that are community-based, with the church as the center of the community.

In preaching the virtues of peace, it is important that the church always be seen as a neutral body. If it is to be effective in its role as a facilitator for healing the continent, its impartiality is crucial. It must truly represent the interests of all of the people.

The Future

The status of women is the most significant issue affecting the well-being of children today. This is true all over the world. As women begin to participate outside the home, they must be better educated. This education extends beyond vocational training to the health sciences and social behavior.

In Africa today, this transition is beginning to take place. As the level of African women's education rises, the number of children they have decreases. Greater access to resources and knowledge about good health and hygiene has had a positive impact on the condition of children.

The acknowledgement of women's legal rights, especially the passage of gender-sensitive inheritance laws in many African countries, is a major achievement. These changes affect the standard of living of children when women become sole providers through divorce or the death of their husbands.

Until Africa comes to peace with herself, the future of African children will continue to look bleak. Unless African leaders act, the various conventions and resolutions they have ratified will remain only paper and will not effectively change the situation for children in Africa. Leaders must set an example for the future leaders of Africa.

As long as there is no peace, limited resources will continue to be diverted from productive social uses, such as health and education, to the destructiveness of war. The health and well-being of society, and of children in particular, will not become a priority until "nationhood" ceases to dominate the minds of African leaders. There is a desperate need to identify nations in terms of human beings. Africa in the 1990s is concerning herself with human development, with developing the human and institutional capacity to design and implement strategies for sustainable development. The most important investment for Africa's future is Africa's children.

The enjoyment of the highest attainable standard of health is one of the fundamental rights of every human being without distinction of race, religion, political belief, economic or social condition.

—*Constitution of the World Health Organization*

•

Then Jesus summoned his twelve disciples and gave them authority over unclean spirits, to cast them out, and to cure every disease and every sickness.

—*Matthew 10:1*

9

Creating the Conditions for Health:
Beyond Medical Issues

Cathie Lyons

The Declaration of Human Rights, Article 25, states:

> Everyone has the right to a standard of living adequate for the health and
> well-being of himself and his family, including food, clothing, housing, medical
> care and necessary social services, and the right to security in the event of un-
> employment, sickness, disability, widowhood, old age or other lack of livelihood in
> circumstances beyond his control. . . .

Countries ratifying the International Covenant on Economic, Social and
Cultural Rights (1976) are urged to take whatever steps necessary for:

- the reduction of the still-birth rate and of infant mortality and for the healthy
  development of the child;
- the improvement of all aspects of environmental and industrial hygiene;
- the prevention, treatment and control of epidemic, endemic, occupational and other
  diseases;
- the creation of conditions which would assure to all medical service and medical
  attention in the event of sickness.

The Alma-Ata Principles

Health is more than a medical issue. Medical missionaries of North American
and Canadian churches have witnessed this firsthand. The concern for health
as "a state of complete physical, mental and social well-being, and not merely
the absence of disease or infirmity," was reaffirmed at the International Conference on Primary Health Care in 1978 in Alma-Ata (now the capital of the
Republic of Kazakhstan, formerly Soviet Kazakhstan). Representatives of 134

CATHIE LYONS is an associate general secretary of the General Board of Global Ministries of
the United Methodist Church, responsible for the Health and Welfare Program Department. In
1985, at the Non-Governmental Forum in Nairobi, she was coordinator for the Plenary Session on
Health. She is the author of *Journey toward Wholeness: Justice, Peace, and Health in an Interdependent
World* (Friendship Press, 1987).

nations also affirmed "Health for All by the Year 2000" as the most important social goal of the world community and cited primary health care as the major strategy for achieving that goal. A significant milestone in world cooperation for health, the conference was cosponsored by the United Nations Children's Fund (UNICEF) and the World Health Organization (WHO).

Created in 1948, the World Health Organization is the specialized agency of the UN responsible for international health matters and offers health professionals of some 189 countries the opportunity to exchange knowledge and experience. To meet the goal of "Health for All" by the year 2000, WHO has urged the UN member states to combine the efforts of various sectors of society (including animal husbandry, agriculture, food, housing, public works, education, and health care) in support of people's health and development.

In the 1978 Alma-Ata Declaration delegates affirmed the importance of clinics, hospitals, and health workers, but also urged governments and communities to address the social, economic, political, and cultural challenges that shape people's daily living conditions and result in high rates of illness and early death from preventable causes. The declaration called for new national health priorities to develop comprehensive health services, including health education and disease prevention programs, as well as curative and treatment services. These new services would be community-based (accessible from where people live and work) and would assure essential services at people's first point of contact with the health care system. Primary health care would be the centerpiece, with all other care levels organized as backup.

The declaration also affirmed that top-to-bottom decision-making should be replaced with community-level participation. The strategies developed should:

- be responsive to the needs of those affected;
- use appropriate technologies;
- build on effective indigenous practices and remedies;
- train and utilize traditional practitioners;
- be provided at prices all could afford; and
- empower people to care for themselves.

It would be essential to minimize dependence on outside resources and supplies if this new community-based approach were to be sustainable.

The Alma-Ata principles are still important, because the vast majority of illnesses affecting newborns, children, youth, and adults are preventable, yet needless suffering, disability, and premature deaths continue unabated. (This is true in the United States and Canada as well as in the developing and least developed nations.)

In the early years of the churches' work in medical mission, doctors and nurses were assigned to areas where vast numbers of people suffered from illnesses that swept entire regions and where little help was available. They developed hospitals and clinics often before the development of comparable government facilities. The establishment of these treatment centers and the dedication of the early medical missionaries remain points of pride in our mission history.

Over time more hospitals, clinics, and field dispensaries were established by governments as well as non-governmental and religious groups. Doctors and nurses worked long hours without adequate supplies, electricity, or clean water to care for the people lined up at their doors. Caring for people through repeated bouts of illness was a never-ending task.

Because the needs were so great, attention initially focused on treatment service facilities and supplies. More health dollars were provided to hospitals, and over time, services became more sophisticated and expensive. Meanwhile, fewer of those needing services could afford care. Although clinics, hospitals, and health centers became the local repositories for knowledge about illness and causation, treatment and prevention, and they fulfilled a vital need in the life of their communities, health workers realized that they were not the total answer. Many people traveled days to get treatment, but thousands more had no way to get to a hospital or preferred to avoid such strange and intimidating places.

The most troubling questions remained. Health care workers still wondered how to

- assist people to avoid illness;
- address on a large scale diseases that could be eliminated through preventive practices;
- reach mothers with information about health for themselves and their children;
- help people gain access to clean water and be responsible for sanitary disposal of human and animal wastes;
- help achieve greater standards of safety (from accidents, animals, and pests);
- help people move beyond poverty and the back-breaking work of providing food and shelter for the family;
- relieve the multiple burdens women carried as mothers, and as the key providers of food, water, fuel, and care for children, families, and the home; and
- help people play a primary role in identifying and addressing their own problems.

The Roots of the Problems

Health workers realized that many illnesses were rooted in daily living conditions, including local attitudes, traditions, and beliefs regarding the roles and

World Health Day

The constitution of the World Health Organization, upholding the right of every human being to achieve the highest attainable standard of health, took effect on April 7, 1948. This date is commemorated each year as World Health Day. Special literature is developed annually for World Health Day celebrations. Program suggestions are made, which can be adapted by schools, religious organizations, and work places as a way of involving community groups, local organizations, and families in programs of health promotion and disease prevention. Also, World AIDS Day is observed every December, as a way of promoting worldwide recognition and local response.

status of males and females. The World Health Organization and UNICEF began working with governments and other organizations, implementing massive programs to reduce the threat of the major childhood diseases, eradicate smallpox, and control malaria and other major communicable illnesses. Infant mortality was reduced in many countries and some contagious diseases were eliminated or better controlled.

In support of UNICEF's emphasis on the benefits of breast-feeding to infants and mothers alike, WHO called on its member states to adopt the international code regarding breast milk substitutes (formulas). This code censures the marketing and promotion of such products by multinational corporations in regions where their use is inappropriate and costly and could add the risk of water-borne diseases to infants whose health is already precarious.

WHO and UNICEF recognized that babies born to healthy mothers had a better start in life and would benefit from better maternal care. Through its Maternal Health and Safe Motherhood Program, WHO works with countries to educate women about their own care, their pregnancies, and the care of their children.

The 1978 Alma-Ata meeting included representatives from countries that had benefited from innovative attempts to address the needs of people living in areas without doctors. China's "barefoot doctor" approach stands out. The Comprehensive Rural Health Project in India's Maharashtra State trains illiterate village women to become health workers and organizes groups to identify and address critical needs of village people. The Feld'sher system (in countries of the former Soviet Union) trains local people to staff and run first aid stations that oversee community health needs. Principles of these successful programs were incorporated into the principles of primary health care adopted at Alma-Ata.

But there were no easy solutions. Medical science had no remedy for illnesses caused by the effects of grinding poverty, lack of access to clean water and good food, unsafe living and working conditions, environmental pollution, unhealthy lifestyles (including use of tobacco and alcohol), unhealthy diets and lack of exercise, civil strife and racism, the denial of basic human rights, and the servitude and low status of females.

These were root causes of illness and poor health status in 1978 and continue to be so today. Any attempt to address the health needs of all peoples must take these root causes into account and provide room for diverse cooperative efforts that give local people primary roles in identifying their own needs, developing strategies to meet those needs, and evaluating progress.

Many years have passed since the goal of "Health for All" was established. Since that time, the WHO has prepared periodic reports on the world health situation for the scientific community and for decision-makers in health care and related sectors. The eighth report, *Implementation of the Global Strategy for Health for All by the Year 2000,* written in 1993, covers progress by 151 countries — 96 percent of the world's population. The excerpt below highlights continuing needs:

> While commitment to the aims of health for all has remained firm, and member states have adopted the primary health care approach as described in the Declaration of Alma-Ata for the development of their health care systems, the implementation of strategies to achieve those aims has, in many cases, slowed down...not only from economic factors, but also from the rigidity of health systems, weak infrastructure, the constraints on achieving real participation by all related sectors and the inadequacy of efforts to promote health and prevent specific health problems....A number of developing countries have retained traditional systems established during former colonial times. The national socio-economic environment has thus not generally been conducive to the development of systems based on [the concept of] primary health care.

In the same report, WHO's director general notes:

> Developing countries have been experiencing...rapid aging of the population, together with an increasing incidence of noncommunicable diseases linked to changes in lifestyle. The growing prevalence of cancer, cardiovascular disease, diabetes and other chronic conditions in addition to the long-standing problems of communicable disease such as cholera, malaria and tuberculosis impose a double burden on health care systems in these countries. There are also worrying trends in mortality from accidents and suicide in young adults, particularly in the developed countries. In addition there is the pandemic of HIV infection and AIDS, which imposes a particularly heavy burden on developing countries. All these realities must be taken into account in implementing public health action geared to achieving the goal of health for all through primary health care.

AIDS

The AIDS pandemic is one of many global health crises for which the World Health Organization has taken leadership, working with national governments and their health programs. Integration of efforts from various sectors of society — such as health, education, and communications — and community-based primary health care strategies, focusing on disease prevention and changes in human behavior — are essential in combating this worldwide health problem.

The World Health Organization held its first meeting on AIDS in 1983 and established its Global Program on AIDS (GPA) in 1987. Six years later, in a paper titled "The HIV/AIDS Pandemic: Global Spread and Global Response" delivered at the ninth International Conference on AIDS, the director stated:

> More than 14 million adolescents and adults have been infected since the start of the pandemic. . . . The largest number of infections is still in sub-Saharan Africa — more than 8 million — but the biggest increase in the past year has been in Latin America and South and South-East Asia, each with 1.5 million or more infections. What has not changed is the basic transmission pattern. Worldwide, about three-quarters of cumulative HIV infections have been acquired through unprotected sexual intercourse . . . and heterosexual transmission is still on the rise. Five out of every eleven newly infected adults are now women. Mother-to-child transmission is also growing in importance. So far, about 1 million infants have been infected via this route.

WHO projects that in each of the final years of this century, the annual number of new AIDS cases will triple, and by the year 2000, 30 to 40 million people worldwide will be infected with HIV. The heavy burden of disease, disability, and loss of human resources will have an extreme effect on the social, political, and economic stability of the developing world. The WHO estimates pale, however, in comparison with a 1993 study by Harvard University's Global AIDS Policy Coalition, which cites a potential for 120 million infections by the year 2000.

WHO estimates that implementing effective prevention strategies in developing countries will cost $1.5 to $2.9 billion each year, but billions more will be saved as a result. According to "The HIV/AIDS Pandemic," cited above:

> If comprehensive prevention were carried out in all developing countries starting now, it could cut the number of new adult infections during the rest of the decade in half — from almost 20 million to 10 million. . . . In purely financial terms, preventing AIDS means averting enormous costs — not only the direct costs of health care, but the far greater indirect costs, especially the income lost because of illness and death. WHO estimates that investing $2.5 billion a year would save

Health for All by the Year 2000

Frequently the question is raised whether the global goal of "Health for All by the Year 2000" can be accomplished, and as the turn of the century nears, the question becomes more distressing. The words of WHO itself are helpful in this regard. In the WHO brochure *Health for All: One Common Goal,* we read:

"Health for All by the Year 2000" does not mean that by then disease and disability will no longer exist, or that doctors and nurses will be taking care of everybody. What it does mean is that resources for health will be evenly distributed, and that essential health care will be accessible to everyone, with full community involvement. It means that health begins at home, in schools and in factories, and that people will use better approaches than they do now, for preventing disease and alleviating unavoidable disease and disability. It means that people will realize that they have the power to shape their own lives and the lives of their families; free from the avoidable burden of disease, and aware that ill-health is not inevitable.

close to $90 billion in direct and indirect costs by the turn of the century [and would assure an] incalculable yield of diminished human suffering.

Such a pandemic requires coordinated global strategy. In January 1994, the United Nations announced plans to combine the AIDS efforts of a number of its agencies (including the Global Program on AIDS) into a unified program to be administered by WHO. This coordinated effort will combine the work currently being done by the United Nations Development Fund and Population Fund, WHO, UNICEF, and UNESCO and is tentatively scheduled to begin in 1996.

Health and the Churches

Through the years, the World Health Organization has placed emphasis on the same urgent health issues and concerns that have often been on the agendas of North American and Canadian churches. These include the critical health needs of women and children, refugees, and other persons displaced from their homelands as a result of racism, civil strife, persecution, or natural disaster.

For many churches, the question of how scarce health dollars should be spent, in an effort to reach the poorest of the poor and those with little or no access to the benefits of scientific medicine, has caused a re-examination of health ministry priorities. How much financial support should be allocated to hospitals and medical programs in areas where governmental programs have been developed? Should medical mission personnel be reassigned? What role might they play in working with communities on health promotion and disease prevention? Some churches are re-emphasizing the primary health care approach as a part of their justice and development programs, recognizing it as a comprehensive strategy for the self-development of individuals and the communities in which they live.

Thus, local churches are seeking to become communities of healing, in keeping with Jesus' teachings about the kingdom of God being established in our midst. With healing miracles, Jesus demonstrated God's compassion and love for the people. Jesus' responsiveness to all who sought his healing touch demonstrated the importance of health and wholeness in the new heaven and earth he had been sent to establish.

New models of church-based care are being developed that encourage individuals to take greater responsibility for their own health and the health of their families. Lay health advisor programs demonstrate the ability of lay persons to learn health promotion and disease prevention techniques that can be imparted to others. Parish nurse programs demonstrate how health care can be provided through congregational efforts to bring health promotion as close as possible to where people live and worship.

Some congregations have developed Covenant to Care statements, making it known in their communities that: "If you have AIDS, or if you are the loved one of a person with AIDS, you are welcome here." WHO's Global Program on AIDS upholds the importance of such acts of acceptance. Without such acceptance, a great deal of denial is perpetuated, and AIDS is seen as a problem existing somewhere else, affecting people who are different.

The current efforts of the churches to focus on the critical health needs of children and youth and on the effects of drug abuse and domestic and street violence on families and entire communities are also important to WHO. Making the world safe for children and other living things is an urgent concern of all nations. The religious sector has an important role to play in addressing violence, ethnic hatred, and racism as root causes of physical, mental, and spiritual suffering that deeply affect the health and wholeness of individuals and communities.

The worldwide goal of "Health for All" can be seen in theological terms as an expression of God's hope for the world. The question is not whether the goal can be achieved, but whether the churches are doing all they can to make the goal a reality.

Humanity stands at a defining moment in history. We are confronted with a perpetuation of disparities between and within nations, a worsening of poverty, hunger, ill health and illiteracy, and the continuing deterioration of the ecosystems on which we depend for our well-being. However, integration of environment and development concerns and greater attention to them will lead to the fulfillment of basic needs, improved living standards for all, better protected and managed ecosystems and a safer, more prosperous future. No nation can achieve this on its own but together we can — in a global partnership for sustainable development.

—from the Preamble to Agenda 21

•

If you follow my statutes and keep my commandments and observe them faithfully, I will give you your rains in their season, and the land shall yield its produce, and the trees of the field shall yield their fruit. Your threshing shall overtake the vintage, and the vintage shall overtake the sowing; you shall eat your bread to the full, and live securely in your land. And I will grant peace in the land, and you shall lie down, and no one shall make you afraid; I will remove dangerous animals from the land, and no sword shall go through your land.

—Leviticus 26:3–6

10

The Environment, the Churches, and the United Nations

David G. Hallman

The UN has finally caught up to the churches in the environment field. This may seem like a pretty outrageous statement given the churches' lateness in recognizing the seriousness of the ecological crisis confronting the world. Environmental groups and some government departments were addressing environmental problems long before the churches. The UN Environment Program has been in existence for many years.

What is new for the UN is the recognition of links between ecological destruction and economic injustice. The 1992 Rio Earth Summit, formally called the UN Conference on Environment and Development (UNCED), brought together concerns about the environment and global poverty. Churches have consciously focused on these linkages for over two decades, particularly through the efforts of the World Council of Churches (WCC). Churches have contributed to the growing awareness of the importance of these connections within the UN system, governments, and non-governmental organizations. In turn, the churches have been enriched by the UNCED process. The future holds significant opportunities for churches to work with the UN in protecting God's creation and bringing about greater justice among the peoples of the Earth.

A Grounding in Theology and Ethics

A Swedish church delegate at the ecumenical gathering sponsored by the WCC during the Earth Summit commented that churches are, or at least

DAVID G. HALLMAN has been the national program officer for environmental concerns with the United Church of Canada for more than fifteen years. He has been extensively involved with the World Council of Churches, most recently on initiatives related to the 1992 Earth Summit, the UN Commission on Sustainable Development, and the issue of climate change. He is the author of numerous books and articles including *Ecotheology: Voices from South and North*, copublished in 1994 by the World Council of Churches and Orbis Books.

should be, good at "internal ecology," the moral and ethical understandings of caring for God's creation. This is one of the exciting areas of growing theological awareness among the churches today, but results, in part, from criticism from outside the church. Some eloquent environmentalists, scientists, historians, and UN diplomats have argued that the Christian tradition must accept a major part of the blame for the destruction of the environment. They point to Bible passages such as Genesis 1:28, where God blessed the newly created humans and gave them "dominion over" all the other beings. They also cite theological writings and church documents that suggest that God has given humans total authority over everything on the Earth to use as we wish for our own human purposes regardless of the consequences. One of the most famous critiques came from American historian Lynn White, Jr., in his essay, "The Historical Roots of Our Ecological Crisis," published in 1967.

Theologians and other Christians, quite shaken by these criticisms, have re-examined the Bible and Christian theology. They have found wondrous sources within Scripture and our theological traditions that point to God's passionate love for all creation and God's call to humans to respect and care for it. Important new ecological understandings have come from stewardship theology (Douglas John Hall), process theology (John Cobb, Jr.), feminist theology (Rosemary Radford Ruether, Sallie McFague), indigenous theology (George Tinker, Stan MacKay), and creation theology (Thomas Berry, Matthew Fox), as well as the writing and preaching of many Christians at a community level.

This theological creativity has influenced the ethical understandings and actions of the churches. The rich outpouring on ecological theology has been coupled with the churches' long tradition of concern for justice within the human community, their international development work with a focus on human and community empowerment, and their challenges to governments, transnational corporations, and international financial institutions that bear significant responsibility for the enormous gap between the rich and the poor in the world.

That gap between the rich and poor does not exist only between nations. Within our rich industrialized countries, many people live in severe poverty. The National Council of the Churches of Christ in the USA and a number of its larger member churches have been in the forefront of the "eco-justice movement" in the United States. This focuses on the connections between environmental and economic injustice (for example, "environmental racism").

Church Contributions to UN Thinking

One would be hard-pressed to draw a direct link, but some pieces of church history have very likely played an important role in the UN's growing awareness of the important connections between environment and development.

One has to do with sustainability. Most people associate the sustainable development concept with the UN task force headed by Norway's Prime Minister Gro Harlem Brundtland, which produced the 1987 report, "Our Common Future: The Report of the World Commission on Environment and Development." The Brundtland Commission and its report led very directly to the convening of the Rio Earth Summit five years later.

But sustainability was being discussed by churches twenty years ago. In 1974, the WCC subunit on Church and Society held a consultation in Bucharest involving scientists, economists, and theologians. They focused on prospects for development, given the increasing demands of high consumption in the rich countries and growing population worldwide. The "limits to growth" debate was raging at this time. The consultation introduced the concept of sustainability, meaning that development should be pursued both in rich and poor countries in a way that could be maintained for the long term both environmentally and economically.

The Bucharest consultation led the 1975 Nairobi Assembly of the WCC to initiate a study on a Just, Participatory and Sustainable Society (JPSS) and to the convening of a major conference in 1979 on "Faith, Science and the Future." This work in turn laid the foundation for a major new program launched at the WCC's Vancouver Assembly in 1983 on "Justice, Peace and the Integrity of Creation."

These programs were sponsored by the WCC and its member churches, but they were occurring within societies coming to grips with the seriousness of the ecological crisis. During the 1980s, governments, non-governmental organizations, and international agencies such as the UN came to realize the ecological crisis could not be resolved by some kind of technological fix. Rather, it had to do with fundamental issues of values and ethics. The churches' discussions of sustainability and the interrelatedness of justice, peace, and creation began to provide some insights about the profound shifts needed in how we live and how we organize our societies and economic systems.

The Rio Earth Summit

Those of us who participated in the UN Conference on Environment and Development (UNCED) in June 1992 came home to discover that many people were deeply cynical about what had happened there. They had seen the television pictures of the U.S. delegation refusing to sign the Biodiversity Convention and being unwilling to include in the Climate Change Convention any specific targets for the reduction of greenhouse gas emissions. They were convinced that the Earth Summit was just a big photo opportunity for world leaders to look as if they were doing something about the environment.

That negative image of UNCED has been a big problem because it masked the profound stories of hope that came out of Rio. Granted, not many of those stories came from the actual government conference. But then, the Earth Summit was a lot more than the government conference. The parallel non-governmental gathering called the Global Forum brought together thirty thousand people from around the world representing environment groups, development organizations, women's networks, youth, peace groups, and religious faiths. In strategy sessions, open forums, dialogues with government delegates, and planning meetings for future collaboration, these groups made considerable progress in linking environment and development.

The WCC convened a special ecumenical gathering at the time. More than 150 Christians from around the world, including representatives from churches in Canada and the United States, met together during the first week at a Catholic Retreat Center in a poor neighborhood of Rio. We prayed and worshiped together and engaged in sessions analyzing the UNCED deliberations. During the second week, we participated with other non-governmental organizations in the activities of the Global Forum. Out of this ecumenical gathering came a report, *Searching for the New Heavens and the New Earth*, which included a Pentecost letter to the member churches of the WCC, an assessment of the UNCED treaties, worship resources, and reports of working groups on the role of churches, theology, education and communication, economics, pollution, militarism and peace, population and environment.

The WCC report from Rio has been translated into various languages and used by churches to interpret what went on at UNCED and what kinds of challenges it presented for the future work of the churches. The task of interpretation and planning has been facilitated by a thirty-minute video, *The Earth Summit: What Next?* produced by the United Church of Canada for the WCC. Churches in Canada and the United States conducted many educational events both before and after the Earth Summit to help their members become more aware of the ethical issues related to environment and development.

A wide range of practical projects has been initiated by non-governmental organizations, including churches. For instance, churches in Canada and in Southeast Asia discovered during the WCC's ecumenical gathering that they had common concerns about unsustainable forestry practices and about the infringement of logging on the well-being of native peoples and indigenous forest dwellers. The churches in Canada and the Philippines decided to convene a gathering that brought together church representatives, environmentalists, and indigenous people from Canada, the Philippines, Malaysia, Indonesia, Viet Nam, Hong Kong, New Zealand, and Taiwan. This consultation on "sustainable forests," held in the Philippines in May 1993, allowed participants to learn more about the churches' involvement in forestry in each other's countries and to initiate various national, regional, and international actions.

Earth Charter

The UN organizers of the Earth Summit had hoped that a ringing declaration about human moral responsibility to care for the Earth, comparable to the UN Declaration on Human Rights, might be one agreement coming out of Rio. In the early planning stages, the UN invited the World Council of Churches to participate in drafting ideas. The WCC hosted an interfaith event in 1991, which produced a statement entitled "One Earth Community." The vision of an Earth Charter, however, did not prevail. Instead, participating governments adopted the "Rio Declaration," which includes twenty-seven principles defining the rights and responsibilities of nations as they pursue human development and well-being.

Nevertheless, the image of humans and the rest of nature being part of "one earth community" is starting to generate interest just as the churches' pioneering concept of sustainability did in the past. The Earth Council, an independent body set up in Costa Rica after UNCED, is leading this effort. The WCC is participating.

There were lots of disappointments and problems with the Earth Summit. But the UN, to its credit, made it dramatically different from previous conferences by opening it up to thousands of ordinary citizens through the Global Forum. Indeed, the whole planning process, the "PrepComs," or Preparatory Committee sessions, over the previous two years, had allowed for a much more intensive NGO involvement than in previous UN gatherings. The rules for NGO participation in the UN system generally are now being revised in light of this positive experience.

An encouraging development since Rio has been the reversal of the U.S. position on the Biodiversity Convention. The U.S. had been the only country to refuse to sign, largely because the Bush administration saw it as a threat to American multinational biotechnology companies. In 1993 the Clinton administration reversed that position and signed the convention.

The convention has now been ratified by a sufficient number of countries to become international law. The first meeting of the "Conference of Parties," the governing council for the convention, was scheduled for 1995.

Climate Change

Of all of the environmental issues on the UNCED agenda, the one in which the World Council of Churches has been most intensively involved is climate change. Perhaps more than any other environmental problem, climate change reflects the severely distorted relationship that has developed between human beings and the rest of creation as well as within the human family.

For decades, there have been massive emissions of greenhouse gases from industrialized nations. The production of carbon dioxide from the burning of fossil fuels for energy production, industry, transportation, and military purposes has grown dramatically since the end of World War II. But it goes back even further. Scientists estimate that about 80 percent of the human-produced carbon dioxide content in the atmosphere comes from the past 150 years of industrialized activity in the countries of North America, Europe, and the former Soviet-bloc nations. Carbon dioxide and the other main greenhouse gases, such as chlorofluorocarbons, or CFCs, methane, and nitrous oxide, are building up a thicker and thicker blanket of gases in the atmosphere, which in turn is trapping increased amounts of heat. Scientists predict that a global warming will result in hotter temperatures and more droughts in large land masses such as sub-Saharan Africa and the midwestern prairies in North America; rising sea levels, which will inundate many coastal and delta areas; and an increase in the frequency and intensity of tropical storms. Millions of environmental refugees will be displaced from their homes.

Climate change represents a threat to the integrity of God's creation and constitutes a major injustice, because the problem is caused largely by the rich nations but the impact will be suffered disproportionately by persons in developing countries. The churches were among the early voices calling upon their respective governments and the UN to begin negotiations for a global climate treaty that could address the problem before it was too late. Prior to Rio, the U.S. administration was opposed to including targets and timetables for reducing greenhouse gas emissions. Church leaders in Canada and the United States joined forces at a meeting in Washington in January 1992 to try to influence the Bush administration.

In addition to monitoring the negotiations on climate change in the UN, the WCC also established the Task Force on Climate Change to press fur-

UN International Days and Weeks

The UN calls attention to various issues by designating an annual day or week for observance. You can promote these global concerns by creating your own special activities. For information contact the Public Inquiries Unit, United Nations, Room GA-57, New York, NY 10017, 212-963-4475. In some cases you may wish to contact the sponsoring agency, noted here in parentheses.

March 8: International Women's Day

March 21: International Day for the Elimination of Racial Discrimination

Beginning March 21: Week of Solidarity with the Peoples Struggling against Racism and Racial Discrimination (UN)

March 22: World Day for Water

March 23: World Meteorological Day (WMO)

April 7: World Health Day (WHO)

May 3: World Press Freedom Day

May 15: International Day of Families

May 17: World Telecommunication Day (ITU)

May 31: World No-Tobacco Day (UN)

June 4: International Day of Innocent Children Victims of Aggression

June 16: Day of the African Child

June 26: International Day against Drug Abuse and Illicit Trafficking

July 11: World Population Day

September 8: International Literacy Day (UNESCO)

3rd Tuesday of September: International Day of Peace (Opening of the UN General Assembly)

Last week of September: World Maritime Day (IMO)

October 1: International Day for the Elderly

1st Monday of October: Universal Children's Day (UNICEF) (date varies) and World Habitat Day (Habitat)

October 9: World Post Day

2nd Wednesday of October: International Day for Natural Disaster Reduction (UN)

October 16: World Food Day

October 17: International Day for the Eradication of Poverty

October 24: United Nations' Day and World Development Information Day (UN)

October 24–30: Disarmament Week

Week of November 11: International Week of Science and Peace (UN)

November 20: Africa Industrialization Day (UN)

November 29: International Day of Solidarity with the Palestinian People

December 1: World AIDS Day

December 5: International Volunteer Day for Economic and Social Development (UN)

December 10: Human Rights Day

ther on the ethical dimensions of the issue. Through a series of regional and international consultations, the WCC produced a major study document, *Accelerated Climate Change: Sign of Peril, Test of Faith*. It provides scientific evidence about climate change, reflects on its theological and ethical dimensions, analyzes strategies for reducing the emissions of greenhouse gases, and discusses the fundamental importance of building community and enriching our spirituality if we are to rectify the imbalance in the relationship between human societies and the rest of the natural world. English, Spanish, German, French, Russian, Chinese, and Indonesian versions are available with Korean, Greek, and Japanese translations in process.

Many UN and government officials as well as non-governmental organizations have expressed appreciation to the WCC for infusing the climate change discussions with ethical considerations. Invitations have increased for the churches to participate in secular gatherings addressing such ethical dimensions as international, intranational, and intergenerational equity. Canadian and U.S. churches have distributed the WCC's study document across their denominations as part of educational programs on climate change as well as to government officials and environmentalists.

The UN Commission on Sustainable Development

The UN Commission on Sustainable Development (CSD) is the principal body mandated to follow up on the implementation of the agreements made at UNCED. Created after the Earth Summit, the CSD meets in full session once a year. At its inaugural meeting in June 1993, the WCC had a delegation composed of representatives from Africa, Asia, Europe, Latin America, and North America to monitor the proceedings, consult with non-governmental organizations, and utilize opportunities to advocate with government delegates, NGO representatives, and UN officials regarding the justice, peace, and integrity of creation dimensions of the issues under discussion. At the 1994 session, the WCC was represented with a delegation including Christa Andrade (Puerto Rico), the Rev. Jose P. M. Cunanan (Philippines), Dr. David Hallman (Canada), Prof. Gunnar Heine (Norway), the Rev. Eszter Karsay (Hungary), Tore Samuelsson (Lutheran World Federation), and the Rev. Rainer Lingscheid (World Council of Churches).

At the CSD, the WCC delegations function as a team meeting daily for reflection and strategy discussions, sharing responsibilities for monitoring the various negotiations, participating collectively in WCC-hosted meetings with participants from other religious bodies, and jointly preparing reports.

Agenda 21, the massive blueprint for how to make development socially, economically, and environmentally sustainable, was negotiated during the preparatory committee meetings prior to Rio and at UNCED itself. The CSD reviews the forty chapters of Agenda 21 on a rotating basis over three-year cycles and negotiates implementation strategies. In 1994, the focus was on health, human settlements, fresh water, toxic chemicals, and hazardous wastes, as well as ongoing issues such as finance and technology cooperation. In 1995, the focus is on land, desertification, forests, and biodiversity.

Desertification was not given sufficient attention at UNCED, despite being of great concern to developing nations, especially in Africa. An agreement was reached to begin negotiations on a desertification convention, however, and the proposed convention has been presented to the UN General Assembly.

Challenges for the Future

The churches and the UN face profound challenges in helping the community of nations address the interlinked crises of ecological destruction and global poverty. However, as this brief historical overview has illustrated, there is considerable background to build upon.

One of the major challenges will be to continue probing the ethical dimensions of issues of environment and development so that changes in human societies will be based on values that truly respect the integrity of all creation and move us toward greater social and economic justice within the human family.

Another challenge is to prevent sustainable development from becoming trapped within bureaucratic structures at national or international levels that would inhibit the passion and energy needed to make the kind of fundamental changes required. A related risk is that the concept might get co-opted by powerful economic interests to legitimize their current unsustainable practices. Churches at local, national, and international levels can play a helpful role by both critiquing the processes of planning on sustainable development and making their own positive contributions. A third challenge is to translate the issues of environment and development to the local community level. The UN system can seem a pretty remote world for many people in local congregations. But the issues of environment and development affect us all whether we're talking about toxic wastes, landfills, the fishing crisis in many parts of the world's oceans, or the carbon dioxide emissions from our cars that contribute to climate change. Without the participation of everyone, from UN delegates to local workers, the needed changes will not occur.

— Afterword —

Justice, Peace and the Integrity of Creation in an Emerging World Order

Janice Love

Breathtaking events of recent years leave us searching for new grounding and fresh categories for understanding the world around us as we continue to pursue justice and peace. The changes seem so remarkable and overwhelming at times that it is important to remind ourselves about institutions and processes that endure. A historical moment is upon us, when we can assess the strengths and weaknesses of our current systems of political economy with fresh eyes and new determination. The role of the United Nations and the community of non-governmental organizations is also of crucial significance.

Despite other changes, two characteristics of the global political economy endure: transnationalization and military-industrial rivalry.

Many refer to transnationalization as growing world interdependence, or the making of a "global village." This increased integration of the world's political economy often means that decisions affecting the nature and quality of economic and political life in communities all over the globe are handled in places quite distant from the communities affected. Such remote control guarantees that community and individual well-being is not given high priority.

Military-industrial rivalry is another feature of a world experiencing rapid change. The most deadly military rivalry the world has ever known (between the United States and the former USSR) has abated, yet regional, local, and ethnic rivalries still wreak massive destruction in Liberia, Somalia, and the former Yugoslavia.

Both transnationalization and military-industrial rivalry lead to competing and contradictory pressures, and both now exhibit signs of enormous stress — perhaps due to the ecological strain they place on the planet. But as they

DR. JANICE LOVE is the moderator of the WCC Commission of the Churches on International Affairs. This essay, extracted from her address at the 1991 Annual UN Conference for Non-governmental Organizations (including churches), rings true today.

UN International Years

1992   International Year of Space

1993   International Year of the World's Indigenous Peoples

1994   International Year of the Family

       International Year of Sport and the Olympic Ideal

1995   United Nations Year for Tolerance

1996   International Year for the Eradication of Poverty

1999   International Year of the Elderly

fail, the impact falls first on the poor and marginalized, many of whom are people of color already bearing the heaviest load. In this scenario, the rich grow richer, the poor grow poorer, the globe is militarized, and we waste the creation around us.

Production, research, and technology for military purposes dominate across the globe, and ecological devastation is also almost universal. Nature suffers wherever creation is considered an expendable resource. Either we rapidly reverse this trend or we accept devastating consequences.

The undermining of human community and local culture is a subtle but no less destructive feature of the current economical situation. Technology offers speedy communications and travel but also fosters centers of control distant from, and indifferent to, local needs. Confronted with such a long list of failures of both capitalism and communism, we must develop new ways of thinking about social and economic life.

The Role of the UN and NGOs

Humans will always need some form of political organization, and nation state governance is not likely to end soon. But the idea of the sovereignty of individual states is anachronistic and within less powerful countries is sometimes used against the poor and oppressed. The UN subscribes to the principle of sovereignty, yet one of its most important contributions is to limit the ability of governments to hide behind the claim of sovereignty when they evade standards of human decency. In this respect the work of the UN Commission on Human Rights is commendable.

Christian churches have not always been at the forefront of social, political, and economic analysis. However the churches and other NGOs are more closely attuned to the needs and capabilities of individuals and communities than governments are. As NGOs, we play a vital role in articulating the concerns of people to governments and to intergovernmental organizations such as the UN. If we are to help chart a course that offers hope and renewal, we in the NGO community have dual tasks. We must continue to challenge forces of destruction, and we must also give concrete demonstrations of how to create a different future for the true development of human community — development that puts people and the environment first.

As organizations with creative capabilities, we can offer alternatives to the dominant national and global models of political economy that have been so destructive. And we can help define and aid in implementing basic standards of economic, social, political, and ecological justice.

A Vision of the New

We in the WCC have no blueprints for the creation of alternative national and global political economies. But we do have substantial clarity about what goals such blueprints should pursue, and we are well-connected to groups all over the globe experimenting in such construction. At the World Convocation on Justice, Peace and the Integrity of Creation held in Seoul, Korea, in 1990, we affirmed that "all forms of human power and authority are accountable to people" and committed ourselves "to support the constructive power of people's movements in their struggle for human dignity and liberation, as well as in achieving just and participatory forms of governments and economic structures."

We affirmed "God's preferential option for the poor" and rejected systems that "create and perpetuate poverty or accept it as inevitable and ineradicable." We committed ourselves to a "just economic order on local, national, regional and international levels," an order that ensures "economic systems and policies which reflect that people come first." We confirmed a commitment to pursue "liberation from foreign debt bondage and the establishment of a just structure of the international financial system."

We affirmed that "people of every race, caste and ethnic group are of equal value. In the very diversity of their cultures and traditions, they reflect the rich plurality of God's creation." We committed ourselves to the "eradication of racism and discrimination on national and international levels for all people."

We affirmed "the creative power given to women to stand for life wherever there is death" and committed ourselves to "resist structures of patriarchy which perpetuate violence against women in their homes and in a society which has exploited their labor and sexuality." We made commitments to "seek ways of realizing a new community of women and men."

We affirmed that "all people have the right to be educated, to tell their own stories, to speak their own convictions and beliefs, to be heard by others and to have the power to distinguish truth from falsehood." We committed ourselves to "create means by which the neglected and vulnerable may learn and the silenced may make themselves heard."

We affirmed that "the only possible basis for lasting peace is justice." We committed ourselves to "a comprehensive notion of security that takes the legitimate interests of all nations and peoples into account"; to the "demilitarization of international relations and the promotion of nonviolent forms of defense"; and to a "culture of active nonviolence as a way to work for justice and liberation."

We affirmed that "the world, as God's handiwork, has its own inherent integrity, that land, waters, air, forests, mountains and all creatures, including humanity, are 'good' in God's sight." We committed ourselves to "resist the claim that anything in creation is merely a resource for human exploitation" and to "conserve and work for the integrity of creation both for its inherent value to God and in order that justice may be achieved and sustained."

The pursuit of justice, peace, and the integrity of creation may be articulated in a different way in your own organizations. Substantial diversity exists among us for mutual enrichment and challenge. Within the community of non-governmental organizations, however, we need to commit and equip ourselves anew to face the task of reconstructing our social, political, economic, and ecological future so as to enhance life, not destroy it. History may not offer other generations the remarkable opportunity presented to us now. Thoughtfully, carefully, and energetically, let us embrace it.

Questions for Reflection

Write the vision; make it plain on tablets, so that a runner may read it.

HABAKKUK 2:2

The following questions are designed to stimulate reflection on the concerns described in this book:

1. How do you see the Christian commitment to witness and mission affirmed in these chapters?
2. What contributions of the ecumenical movement in UN activities would you celebrate?
3. What actions or involvements of the ecumenical movement must be continued? discontinued?
4. What new actions and involvements should the ecumenical movement initiate?
5. Consider chapter 5, "Building the Conditions for Peace: Beyond the Blue Helmets." What do we do when the new face of war is within states, between different ethnic, linguistic, religious, or cultural groups, and about intolerance?
6. Consider chapter 6, "Human Rights Is Everybody's Business." How will we work for social, political, economic, and gender rights?
7. Consider chapter 7, "Social Reconstruction: Toward New Roles for Women." What changes in institutions and attitudes are necessary to realize equality between women and men?
8. Consider chapter 8, "Promises to the Children of the World: Africa's Children." Who will guarantee the rights of all the world's children to a good future? How will we keep the promise of life in its fullness to the smallest and most fragile among us?
9. Consider chapter 9, "Creating the Conditions for Health: Beyond Medical Issues." What are the basic health rights that each of us may claim? How will we provide health care to all peoples?
10. Consider chapter 10, "The Environment, the Churches, and the United Nations." What needs to happen for our environment to thrive? How should development be implemented to ensure the life of future generations of the earth?

The churches in both the United States and Canada will be looking for ways to work with the United Nations in the next fifty years. Let your denomination or your Council of Churches know how you feel about these issues — and what visions you have of better ways for the international community to work and for the churches to relate.

Glossary of Terms
and Abbreviations

adjusted progress: national economic progress set back or "adjusted" locally, due to impact of external debt interests and penalties.

appropriate technologies: technologies suited to the population, state of development, and the environment.

Blue Helmets: UN Peacekeeping Forces (so nicknamed because they wear blue helmets).

CAT: Committee Against Torture.

CEDAW: Convention on the Elimination of All Forms of Discrimination Against Women.

CERD: Convention on the Elimination of All Forms of Racial Discrimination.

CESCR: Convention on Economic, Social and Cultural Rights.

CHR: Commission on Human Rights.

Cold War: undeclared ideological conflict between the USSR and the United States, 1945–91.

convention: international treaty covering one issue, such as the International Convention on the Rights of the Child.

conventional war: "hot" or shooting war, involving traditional, limited weaponry.

covenant: international treaty covering several issues, such as the Covenant on Economic, Social and Cultural Rights.

CRC: Convention (or Committee) on the Rights of the Child.

CSD: Commission on Sustainable Development.

Earth Summit: UN Conference on Environment and Development (UNCED) in Brazil in 1992.

economic/structural adjustment: economic setback within developing countries resulting from World Bank and/or International Monetary Fund loan interest and penalties.

ECOSOC: Economic and Social Council of the United Nations.

enter into force: become part of International Law (for UN member states).

gender awareness training: training to create awareness of discriminatory gender practices and social concepts.

gender perspective: a point of view on issues that takes into account gender bias.

General Assembly: Main UN body including representatives of all member states.

HDI: Human Development Index; combines the indicators of longevity or life expectancy, knowledge or educational attainment, and standard of living or income.

HRC: Human Rights Committee.

League of Nations: world peace organization pre-dating the UN.

marginalized: refers to people who cannot get access to the political process, have reduced survival capacity, and are exploited socially and/or economically.

NGO: non-governmental organization (local, national, or international group representing specific constituencies and/or concerns and interests) that is accredited to the UN.

nuclear war: "hot" (active) war, using nuclear weapons.

OAU: Organization of African Unity, founded in 1963.

political will: public and/or governmental energy to support a specific course of action.

Population Fund (UNPFA): UN agency addressing world population issues.

PrepCom: UN Preparatory Committee set up to develop the agenda and the document (Declaration and Plan of Action) for a UN world conference.

rapporteur: individual appointed by the UN Human Rights Commission to collect data and report on specific human rights violations.

Security Council: major UN body with the primary responsibility for maintaining international peace and security.

social reconstruction: reconstruction of social values to create equal conditions for all.

State, nation state, member state: UN terms for countries and country members.

sustainable development: development that does not harm the environment or deplete the earth's natural resources and is technologically appropriate to the situation.

transnationalization: expansion beyond national borders (for example, multinational business), resulting in various impacts at local levels around the globe.

treaty: agreement (also "convention" or covenant in UN terminology).

UNCED: United Nations Conference on Environment and Development; also known as the Earth Summit.

UNDP: United Nations Development Program.

UNESCO: United Nations Educational, Scientific and Cultural Organization.

UNICEF: United Nations Children's Fund (originally set up as the UN International Children's Emergency Fund).

UNIFEM: United Nations Development Fund for Women.

WCC: World Council of Churches.

WHO: World Health Organization.

xenophobia: fear or hatred of strangers or foreigners.

— Appendix —

The United Nations System

Origins of the United Nations

The United Nations came into being on October 24, 1945. Several international meetings and agreements provided the underpinnings of the UN Charter.

- **Atlantic Charter, 1941.** Peace proposal designed by U.S. President Franklin Roosevelt and Britain's Prime Minister Winston Churchill, which sought to ensure security and economic opportunity for all nations.
- **Declaration of the United Nations, 1942.** Document signed by forty-seven nations in support of the Atlantic Charter. The term "United Nations," suggested by President Roosevelt, makes its first appearance.
- **Dumbarton Oaks Conference, 1944.** Meeting of representatives of the United States, the United Kingdom, the Soviet Union, and China in Washington, D.C., at which the first blueprint of the UN was prepared.
- **Yalta Conference, 1945.** Meeting of leaders of the United States, the Soviet Union, and the United Kingdom at which the details of the organization were hammered out.
- **San Francisco Conference, 1945.** Gathering of fifty nations to complete a charter for the UN. The charter was signed on June 26 and entered into force on October 24, which we now celebrate as UN Day. (Poland had yet to form a post-war government and could not attend but signed the charter later as an original member.) Representatives of forty-two non-governmental organizations attended the San Francisco Conference as advisors to the U.S. delegation.

UN Structure

The United Nations has six main bodies. All except the International Court of Justice have headquarters in New York City:

United Nations Headquarters
New York, NY 10017
Tel: 212-963-1234

Reprinted with permission from *ABCs of the U.N.*, copublished by the National Education Association of the U.S. and the United Nations Association of the USA.

THE UNITED NATIONS SYSTEM

● Principal organs of the
  United Nations

● Other United Nations
  organs

○ Specialized agencies
  and other autonomous
  organizations within
  the system

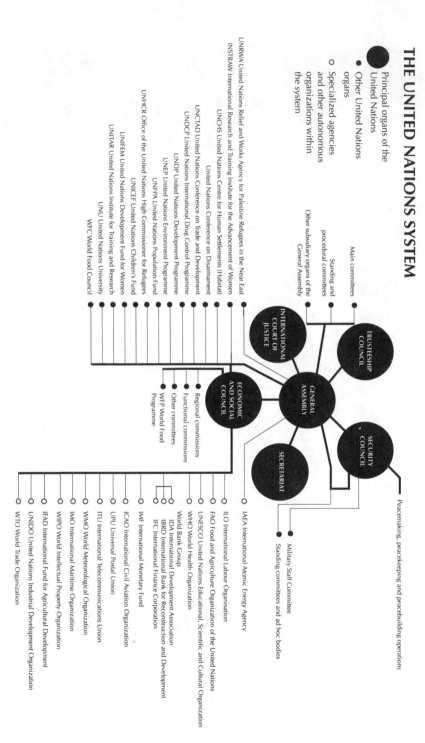

UNRWA United Nations Relief and Works Agency for Palestine Refugees in the Near East
INSTRAW International Research and Training Institute for the Advancement of Women
UNCHS United Nations Centre for Human Settlements (Habitat)
United Nations Conference on Disarmament
UNCTAD United Nations Conference on Trade and Development
UNDCP United Nations International Drug Control Programme
UNDP United Nations Development Programme
UNEP United Nations Environment Programme
UNFPA United Nations Population Fund
UNHCR Office of the United Nations High Commissioner for Refugees
UNICEF United Nations Children's Fund
UNIFEM United Nations Development Fund for Women
UNITAR United Nations Institute for Training and Research
UNU United Nations University
WFC World Food Council

Main committees

Standing and
procedural committees

Other subsidiary organs of the
General Assembly

INTERNATIONAL COURT OF JUSTICE

TRUSTEESHIP COUNCIL

ECONOMIC AND SOCIAL COUNCIL

GENERAL ASSEMBLY

SECURITY COUNCIL

SECRETARIAT

WFP World Food
Programme

Other committees

Functional commissions

Regional commissions

Peacemaking, peacekeeping and peacebuilding operations

● Military Staff Committee
● Standing committees and ad hoc bodies

○ IAEA International Atomic Energy Agency
○ ILO International Labour Organisation
○ FAO Food and Agriculture Organization of the United Nations
○ UNESCO United Nations Educational, Scientific and Cultural Organization
○ WHO World Health Organization
○ World Bank Group
   IDA International Development Association
   IBRD International Bank for Reconstruction and Development
   IFC International Finance Corporation
○ IMF International Monetary Fund
○ ICAO International Civil Aviation Organization
○ UPU Universal Postal Union
○ ITU International Telecommunications Union
○ WMO World Meteorological Organization
○ IMO International Maritime Organization
○ WIPO World Intellectual Property Organization
○ IFAD International Fund for Agricultural Development
○ UNIDO United Nations Industrial Development Organization
○ WTO World Trade Organization

General Assembly (GA). The Assembly is the main deliberative body of the UN. Representatives of all member governments meet for approximately three months each fall to consider reports from the five other bodies, make recommendations on a wide range of international questions, approve the UN budget, and apportion expenses. Each member has one vote. Most decisions are made by simple majority or consensus, although the charter states that resolutions on "important" questions (among them, the maintenance of peace and security and the admission or expulsion of members) require a two-thirds vote. On the recommendation of the Security Council, the GA appoints the Secretary General.

Security Council (SC). The UN Charter gives the Security Council primary responsibility for maintaining international peace and security, and the SC alone has the power to back up its declarations with actions to ensure compliance. Five of the Council's fifteen members are designated permanent members: the United States, Russia (which assumed the Soviet Union's seat in 1992), the United Kingdom, France, and China. The other ten are elected by the GA for a term of two years. Passage of a resolution requires "yes" or abstention votes by all of the five permanent members, plus four additional members, for a total of nine votes.

Secretariat. Headed by the Secretary General, the Secretariat services the UN's main bodies and administers the policies and projects established by them. Its twenty-five thousand men and women from over 150 countries work at the UN headquarters in New York and in Geneva, Vienna, and various places around the world. The Secretary General is appointed for a five-year term and is eligible for reappointment. The post has been held by Boutros Boutros-Ghali of Egypt since 1992.

Economic and Social Council (ECOSOC). ECOSOC coordinates the economic and social work of the UN, its specialized agencies, and its related institutions. It also oversees five regional economic commissions, a number of functional commissions responsible for specific issue areas such as human rights, the status of women, population, and sustainable development, and a few standing committees such as that on non-governmental organizations. ECOSOC's fifty-four members are elected by the GA for three-year terms. It generally holds one four- to five-week session each year, alternating between New York and Geneva.

Trusteeship Council (TC). With a roster of permanent members identical to the Security Council's, the TC originally had jurisdiction over eleven former colonies. Its agenda has been eliminated because all trust territories have achieved independence. Palau became the 185th member of the UN on December 15, 1994.

International Court of Justice (ICJ). The ICJ, known as the World Court, decides legal disputes between countries that agree to accept its jurisdiction. It also can issue advisory opinions at the request of the GA and the SC. The court's fifteen judges, elected by the GA and SC for nine-year terms, are chosen on the basis of qualification, not of nationality, although the principal legal systems of the world must be represented. The ICJ sits at The Hague, Netherlands.

Subsidiary Organs
Created by the General Assembly

The General Assembly has responded to a variety of economic and social needs by creating special bodies to deal with them. Some are funded through the UN regular budget, while others are financed by the voluntary contributions of governments (and sometimes of private citizens). All report to the GA and/or ECOSOC. The dates of the founding resolutions are noted in parentheses. The address, telephone, or fax number of any of these organizations may be obtained from the United Nations Public Inquiries Unit, Room GA-57, New York, NY 10017; 212-963-4475.

UNDRO: Office of the UN Disaster Relief Coordinator (1971). Geneva, Switzerland. A clearinghouse for information on relief needs when earthquakes, floods, hurricanes, and other natural disasters strike. Mobilizes and coordinates emergency assistance from around the world.

UNHCR: Office of the UN High Commissioner for Refugees (1949). Geneva, Switzerland. Provides protection and material assistance to refugees (except those in the Middle East, who are aided by UNRWA) and negotiates with governments to resettle or repatriate them.

Habitat: UN Centre for Human Settlements (1977). Nairobi, Kenya. Deals with housing and related problems of the urban and rural poor in developing countries.

UNICEF: UN Children's Fund (1946). New York. Provides technical and financial assistance to developing countries for programs to benefit children and mothers, targeting (among other areas) nutrition, water and sanitation, education, and maternal and child health.

UNCTAD: UN Conference on Trade and Development (1964). Geneva, Switzerland. Works to standardize principles of international trade and to establish agreements that stabilize commodity prices.

UNIFEM: UN Development Fund for Women (1976). New York. An autonomous agency associated with UNDP that supports projects benefiting low-income women in developing countries.

UNDP: UN Development Program (1965). New York. With its network of offices in developing countries, the UN system's central funding, planning, and coordinating agency for technical cooperation.

UNEP: UN Environment Programme (1972). Nairobi, Kenya. Monitors significant changes in the environment and works to develop environmentally sound development practices worldwide.

UNFPA: UN Population Fund (1967). New York. The largest internationally funded source of assistance to population programs in developing nations. Helps these nations to gather demographic data and to prepare and implement population programs, including family planning.

UNITAR: UN Institute for Training and Research (1963). New York. Seeks to enhance the effectiveness of the UN through training programs for government and UN officials and research on a variety of international issues.

UNRWA: UN Relief and Works Agency for Palestine Refugees in the Near East (1949). Vienna, Austria. Provides education, health, and welfare assistance to Palestinian refugees in Jordan, Lebanon, Syria, the West Bank, and Gaza.

INSTRAW: UN International Research and Training Institute for the Advancement of Women (1976). Santo Domingo, Dominican Republic. Carries out research, training, and information activities to examine, monitor, and enhance the role of women in development.

UNU: UN University (1972). Tokyo, Japan. An autonomous academic institution with a worldwide network of associated institutions, research units, scholars, and fellows but no faculty or degree students of its own.

WFC: World Food Council (1974). A thirty-six-nation body that meets annually at the ministerial level to review major issues affecting the world food situation.

WFP: World Food Programme (1961). Rome, Italy. Jointly sponsored by the UN and the Food and Agriculture Organization. WFP supplies emergency food relief and food aid to support development projects.

Specialized Agencies and Related Organizations

The following autonomous intergovernmental agencies — each with its own charter, budget, and staff — are related to the United Nations by special agreements and are referred to as part of the "UN family." Virtually all these bodies make their annual reports available to the GA and ECOSOC. (The date on which the agency's articles of agreement was signed is noted in parentheses.)

FAO: Food and Agriculture Organization (1945). Rome, Italy. Helps governments to improve the production, processing, marketing, and distribution of food and agricultural products; to promote rural development; and to eliminate hunger. Its Global Information and Early Warning System identifies countries threatened by food shortages.

IBRD: International Bank for Reconstruction and Development (1944). Washington, D.C. Better known as the World Bank. Lends money and provides technical assistance for agriculture and rural development projects as well as projects to develop the country's infrastructure (energy, ports, power facilities, roads, railways, etc.). The Bank incorporates the IDA and the IFC.

IDA: International Development Association (1960). Washington, D.C. Makes loans on easy (or concessional) terms to the poorest of the developing nations.

IFC: International Finance Corporation (1955). Washington, D.C. Assists private enterprise in developing countries.

ICAO: International Civil Aviation Organization (1944). Montreal, Canada. Objective is the safe and orderly growth of civil aviation throughout the world. Sets international safety standards, recommends performance standards for air and ground crews, and formulates rules of the air.

IFAD: International Fund for Agricultural Development (1974). Rome, Italy. Seeks to end hunger and malnutrition in developing countries by helping them improve food production. Makes loans and grants to projects that promote agriculture, livestock development, irrigation, and fisheries.

ILO: International Labour Organisation (1919). Geneva, Switzerland. Established as an autonomous body under the Versailles Peace Treaty. Seeks to improve working conditions, sets international labor standards, and assists member countries in such areas as vocational training, occupational health and safety, and social security.

IMO: International Maritime Organization (1948). London, England. Promotes cooperation among governments on technical matters affecting shipping and sets standards for maritime safety, efficient navigation, and the prevention and control of pollution from ships.

IMF: International Monetary Fund (1944). Washington, D.C. Seeks to promote international monetary cooperation and to facilitate the expansion of trade. Provides financing to countries with balance of payment difficulties and technical assistance to help them improve economic management.

ITU: International Telecommunication Union (1865). Geneva, Switzerland. Formerly the International Telegraph Union. Allocates the radio frequency spectrum and assigns a position to geostationary satellites. Fosters the creation and improvement of telecommunication networks in developing countries.

UNESCO: UN Educational, Scientific and Cultural Organization (1946). Paris, France. Promotes collaboration among nations in the fields of education, science, culture and communications. Trains teachers and education planners; organizes scientific explorations; encourages the preservation of cultural treasures, both natural and humanmade; and assists developing countries in improving their communications media.

UNIDO: UN Industrial Development Organization (1966). Vienna, Austria. Promotes the industrialization of developing countries. Facilitates the transfer of technology to these countries, helps them obtain external financing, and organizes training programs for workers and managers.

UPU: Universal Postal Union (1874). Berne, Switzerland. Regulates international mail delivery, standardizes postal services, and provides training and expert advice to postal systems in developing countries.

WHO: World Health Organization (1946). Geneva, Switzerland. Promotes and coordinates research and programs that advance the cause of disease prevention and primary health care. Provides technical assistance to improve national health education, nutrition, water and sanitation, and maternal and child health; conducts immunization campaigns, and currently coordinates a global program to control (and conquer) AIDS.

WMO: World Meteorological Organization (1951). Geneva, Switzerland. Promotes the international exchange of weather information. Its World Weather Watch coordinates information gained from land stations and space satellites, facilitating extended weather forecasting for the entire globe.

GATT: General Agreement on Tariffs and Trade (1947). Geneva, Switzerland. The principal international entity concerned with the reduction of trade barriers, the conciliation of trade disputes, and international trade relations. GATT is not an organization but a series of multilateral agreements and a forum for developing the rules of trade. It is legally distinct from the specialized agencies.

IAEA: International Atomic Energy Agency (1956). Vienna, Austria. Guides the development of peaceful uses of atomic energy, establishes standards for nuclear safety, and fosters the exchange of scientific and technical information on atomic energy. Established "under the aegis of the UN," it is not a "specialized agency" per se.

UNDCP: UN International Drug Control Programme. Vienna, Austria. Purpose is to enhance the effectiveness and efficiency of the UN structure for drug abuse control, in keeping with the functions and mandates of the UN in this field.

WIPO: World Intellectual Property Organization (1967). Geneva, Switzerland. Promotes acceptance of treaties and agreements protecting intellectual property, such as patents, trademarks, industrial designs, and copyrights.